SpringerBriefs in Economics

More information about this series at http://www.springer.com/series/8876

Alka Parikh

Risks in Agriculture

Farmers' Perspective

Springer

Alka Parikh
Dhirubhai Ambani Institute of Information
and Communication Technology
Gandhinagar, Gujarat
India

ISSN 2191-5504 ISSN 2191-5512 (electronic)
SpringerBriefs in Economics
ISBN 978-981-10-6270-4 ISBN 978-981-10-6271-1 (eBook)
DOI 10.1007/978-981-10-6271-1

Library of Congress Control Number: 2017950030

Printed on acid-free paper

This Springer imprint is published by Springer Nature
The registered company is Springer Nature Singapore Pte Ltd.
The registered company address is: 152 Beach Road, #21-01/04 Gateway East, Singapore 189721, Singapore

About the Book

This book examines the risks involved in agriculture from the farmer's perspective. It investigates the issues that concern farmers the most like why farmers are not increasing the acreage allotted to pulses despite major increases in the price. Primarily based on focused group discussions (FGDs) and individual interviews, it also analyzes the productivity levels for 18 crops using data from eleven districts in several Indian states.

The main risks that farmers face can be divided into two categories—production risks and price risks—and fluctuations in either one can lead to uncertainty in terms of revenues, and at times to considerable losses. The book demonstrates that agricultural productivity, especially in India's semi-arid tropics, leaves much to be desired when compared with other nations. It offers a unique and valuable resource, not only for agriculture economics researchers and all those interested in agriculture, but also anyone seeking to understand current trends in acreage for various crops, fluctuating production levels for different crops, price fluctuations, and farmers' views on allotting acreage and crop insurance.

Contents

About the Author

Alka Parikh is a Professor of Development Economics at Dhirubhai Ambani Institute of Information and Communication Technology. She holds a Ph.D. from Cornell University, USA, and has contributed to working groups of the Planning Commission for the 11th and 12th Five Year Plans. She is on the board of two NGOs, Utthan and Uplift India, and is also on the governing board of the Centre for Social Studies, Surat. Further, she serves on the advisory committee of the Small Grants Program, United Nations Development Program (UNDP). Throughout her career, Prof. Parikh has worked with NGOs, the corporate sector and academic sector to contribute to the field of development studies.

Chapter 1
Introduction

1.1 Risks in Agriculture

E.O. Heady, considered by many as the father of agriculture economics, once said that if you cannot take risks, you should not be in agriculture. It is true that human beings have far less control over agriculture production compared to industrial production, because some of the most important factors affecting the sector are natural factors, beyond the control of humans. Agriculture is a risky business.

But agriculture supplies food, the most important necessity of life. Therefore, governments all over the world try to support agriculture and try to protect it against risks. The most important risks that the farmer faces can be divided into two categories: (i) Production risks and (ii) Price risks. Fluctuations in these two lead to uncertainty in incomes and at times considerable losses for the farmers.

An average Indian farmer faces large risks. Raju and Chand (2010) summarize the main risks that agriculture face: "Agriculture production and farm incomes in India are frequently affected by natural disasters such as droughts, floods, cyclones, landslides and earthquakes. Vulnerability of agriculture production to these disasters is compounded by the outbreak of epidemics and man made disasters such as fire; sale of spurious seeds, fertilizers and pesticides; and price crashes, etc. All these events severely affect farmers through loss in production and farm income and they are beyond the control of the farmers". The National Agriculture Policy 2000 seems to think on the same lines and recognizes price fluctuation and natural calamities as main factors imparting instability to condition of farmers.

A. Parikh, *Risks in Agriculture*, SpringerBriefs in Economics,
DOI 10.1007/978-981-10-6271-1_1

1.2 Risk Proofing Measures

The intensity of variability in yields and resultant uncertainty of incomes is of high concern because overwhelming majority of farmers in India is economically deprived. Most farmers do not have any effective measures to deal with such risks. Jodha (1980) argues that individual risk proofing measures are relatively ineffective in reducing risks in farming. He reaches this conclusion by observing that most such strategies consist of decrease in consumption, selling assets, out migration, etc. All of these leave the farmer in a worse condition than before and hence their capacity to bear risks reduces; it does not increase. Binswanger (1980), reports, using the data of ICRISAT villages, that most such mechanisms of farmers are very expensive in terms of the harm caused.

Thus government support is required to protect the farmers. Various policies have been designed in India for this purpose. To address the price risks and ensure some income stability for the farmers, minimum support prices are declared for 25 crops. The state governments can support more crops under MSP, if the need arises. Forward contracts are also found in certain commodity markets like forward contracts with gin mills for cotton farmers, with sugar factories for sugarcane farmers, etc. Regulated markets have been established in almost all towns to ensure fair prices to the farmers.

The yield risks are addressed by crop insurance. Dandekar (1976) pointed out that although individual insurance is the ideal way to deal with the production risks, it is impractical in Indian situation. To measure how much crop was standing on each field before the disaster is impossible to know. To put it in his words, "it would be administratively difficult, highly expensive, liable to interminable disputes and fraught with grave dangers of moral hazard". India adopted the area approach for insuring crops, based on the Dandekar Committee Report (Dandekar 1976).

1.3 How Effective Is Insurance as a Risk Proofing Measure?

Just 16% farmers in India are covered (Mahul and Stutley 2010) under crop insurance. Just about 3% of the total agriculture holdings of the country are covered under National Agriculture Insurance Scheme. There are just seven–eight states where the scheme works well; the rest of the country has hardly been covered. There is hardly any state where there is continuous coverage of the farmers—there are sudden jumps and sudden falls every year. The number of small and marginal farmers covered is almost double of the number of medium and large farmers covered. But more than 90% of the insured farmers are loanee farmers. Often, they do not even know that they are insured. In spite of this, the claim-premium ratio is 3.25—making the scheme unviable (Vyas and Singh 2006).

Nair (2010) reports that the greatest disadvantage of yield insurance is the delayed claims settlement procedure (it takes at least a year). Thus the whole purpose of insurance is lost. She feels that the weather-based crop insurance scheme is of more relevance to the farmers. Around 10 lakh farmers were insured when the article was written, Rs. 147 crores were paid for claim settlement. Claims disbursed are 2.4 times the premium paid by the farmers so it is beneficial to them. The total premium paid to the insurer includes farmer's share and subsidy paid by the government. The claim-premium ratio works out to be beneficial to the insurer. With government subsidy, this system becomes viable. However, its reach is still very limited. It remains to be seen how viable the scheme would be once more farmers join and become aware of the benefits.

1.4 Understanding the Risks and Farmers' Behavior

The general concern shared by the policy makers as well as the researchers is such low level of insurance coverage for farmers. As mentioned earlier, 90% of the insured farmers are loanee farmers who were insured compulsorily. Voluntary enrollment in the scheme is small. Is it because the farmers are not aware of the benefits or is there some other reason for it? Another relevant question to be asked is: Does the insurance cover the risks that the farmers perceive to be major threats?

We decided to look into these issues by first examining what seem to be the main risks that farmers face—production or price, by analyzing the secondary data. Many studies have done this before (Nadkarni and Deshpande 1982; Mahendradev 1987) but the whole purpose then was to study the trends and not to construct a risk profile. Thus Nadkarni and Deshpande looked at the possible impact of rainfall and Mahendradev studied the trends in fluctuations over time. Hazell (1982) had shown how the improved seed-/fertilizer-based technologies has not contributed much to increase production instability.

The main purpose of this study is to understand the whole list of problems that the farmers feel affect their crop production and increase the instability. We need to know the issues involved from the point of view of the growers, the people who actually face the risks. Analysis of secondary data for this study was done just to understand the extent of uncertainties involved. The main aim is to understand from the farmers the risks that led to these fluctuations. Therefore we interviewed farmers to find out what risks were faced by them most frequently. The risk profile was constructed based on their observations and responses.

The farmers' views were also sought on crop insurance and minimum support price. The purpose was two-fold: (i) to understand whether the risk proofing measures offered are helping the farmers and (ii) to check whether the these risk proofing measures address the main risks that are faced by the farmers.

Chapter 2
About the Study

2.1 Secondary Data

This study is based on both secondary and primary data. The secondary data on area production and yields was collected from government websites. The data for international comparison was collected from various websites—the FAO data bank was particularly useful. The price data was also collected by similar means. Data was usually collected for 10 years. We could not find district level data beyond 2011–2012 for some districts; for other districts it was available till 2013–2014. This data was used to decipher the trends in area, production, and yield as well as the extent of volatility in prices.

2.2 Primary Data Collection

In addition to the secondary data, farmers' responses were collected from 11 districts. Surveys were carried out by 11 B.Tech students of DAIICT in their own home districts. Six districts were from Gujarat (where the Institute is located): Anand and Kheda from central Gujarat (known as prosperous regions), Valsad and Surat from South Gujarat (favorable agricultural factors: soil, rains, etc.), Sabarkantha from Northern Gujarat (traditionally a backward region but developing fast in some parts), and Junagadh from west Gujarat (agriculturally advanced region).

Five districts were from other states: Indore (a semi-arid region), Simla (a hilly region), Jodhpur (arid region), Goa (a coastal region with good rains and soil; also more educated), and East Godavari (agriculturally advanced region). A limited amount of information was available for Kanpur and Ahmedabad that is included here and there but the main findings are from the 11 districts mentioned above.

A. Parikh, *Risks in Agriculture*, SpringerBriefs in Economics,
DOI 10.1007/978-981-10-6271-1_2

The main methods used for survey was focused group discussions (FGDs) and individual interviews. Usually the FGDs had seven–eight participants, not more. It is true that such discussions are usually dominated by a few but that does not mean that others are not participating. They show their agreement or disagreement by either nodding or looking slightly uncomfortable. So a pointed question can be asked to them to understand their view point. Also, they would generally discuss the responses among themselves and then the vocal one would voice these opinions. The only thing that we ensured was to hold the discussions of the large and small farmers separately to take care of the social dominance problem. The questionnaires were all semi-structured.

The individual interviews helped in getting further insights into the farmers' experiences wherein the farmers shared their beliefs and problems in more details.

2.3 Sample Size and Villages Surveyed

Three main crops from each sample districts were identified (the area under each crop was noted and the crops were ranked based on the area cultivated) and taken up for the study. Totally 18 crops were analyzed for this study.

The villages were selected based on two criteria: (a) where some of these major crops were grown and (b) where some known link person could be found to facilitate the survey. However, the methodology differed a little in Jodhpur. Farmers from various villages had gathered for some function. All the interviews and FGDs were conducted there. In Surat, a group of 10 farmers from different villages was interviewed when they had come for Krishi Sabha. The rest were interviewed from the villages, using the above criteria.

514 farmers were surveyed from the 11 districts. Out of these, 371 were small and marginal and 118 were large farmers (The land size of 25 was missed out during the group discussions). In addition, 72 farmers from Kanpur and 57 farmers from Ahmedabad district had participated in group discussions held by other two student researchers. Thus totally 643 farmers contributed their views for this study.

The villages surveyed were as follows:

Anand (26 farmers): Chikhodra, Rasnol, Boriyavi, Samarkha
Simla (58 farmers): Sarahan, Mashobra, Adyeog, Rohru, Ghannati
Sabarkantha (51 farmers): Chhadarda and Hadiyol from Prantij Tehsil, Juna Chamu and Kothan from Vadali tehsil
Indore (49 farmers): Sitapar, Jamli, Naded, Rau
Surat and Tapi (45 farmers): In Surat: Haripura, Kadod and Bhatlav (Bardoli tehsil), Kharoli and Naren (Mandavi Tehsil)
In Tapi: Andhatri, Vadiya, Bhajipura, Delvada and Mordevi (Valod Tehsil), Kelkui, Palasiya, Ambia, Khutadiya, Vandardevi and Dhajamba (Vyara tehsil)
Valsad (27 farmers): Umarsadi, Kanjan, Samarpada, Khaprada
Jodhpur (68 farmers): Virawas, Rupawas, Birawas, Hariara

Junagadh (57 farmers): Ambecha (Maliya Hatina Taluk) Jhinjhuda and Kenedipur (Mendarda Taluk)
Goa (61 farmers): Chimbel, Talaigaon and Nerul (Tiswadi Taluk), Calangute and Assagao (Bardez Taluk), Benaulim (Salcete Taluk)
East Godavari (35 farmers): Amalapuram, Sannavilli (Uppalaguptam Mandal), Kakinada and Fakruddinpalem (Pithapuram Mandal)
Kheda (37 farmers): Khumarvaad, Umiya Farm, Bavaralaat.

2.4 Limitation of the Study

This paper undertakes quantitative analysis for the secondary data only. The primary data has been analyzed mainly using qualitative parameters. This is because the primary data is based on projects done by different students. There are differences in data contents that make is difficult to undertake quantitative analysis.

Chapter 3
Examining Fluctuations: Analysis of District Level Data

3.1 Introduction

The secondary data on area, production, and yield for eighteen crops were collected. Since production is equal to area multiplied by yield, any change in the two variables can cause a change in total production. How much acreage to devote for a crop is farmers' decision, but how much production actually comes out of the field is decided by many factors like, the technology used, the availability and quality of inputs, and the weather. In other words, fluctuations in crop area show the farmers' choices and preferences. It is not risk; it is rather a risk proofing measure—if you feel that productivity or price of a particular crop might fall, you allocate the field area to some other crop. Fluctuations in yields reveal the production risks that farmers face while cultivating. Thus to understand the extent of production risks for each crop, we have studied the yield fluctuations.

We feel that the fluctuations in yields tend to come down as the farmer masters the technology. Our belief is based on the fact that nations that are at the forefront of agriculture technology also tend to have more stable production. Learning to use the technology properly seems to be an important determining factor for risk reduction, although it is not the only factor.

Resource availability, especially access to irrigation, can also affect the yield fluctuations—farmers dependent solely on rains tend to have much more fluctuations in production than farmers having an alternative source of water.

At the same time, a certain risk component always remains because the production is dependent on natural factors that no one can control. This would be evident from the fluctuations experienced by the leading nations. When we compare

---

This chapter is based on the research reports for different districts written by 11 BTech students: Kheda: Valay Vaidya, Anand: Kartikaya Chaturvedi, Surat: Divyesh Chaudhary, Jodhpur: Amit Aseri, Sabarkantha: Rahul Gajjar, Simla: Vivek Kumar Bodh, Indore: Parth Dave, Junagadh: Sandip Ravaliya, Goa: Shashank Singh, Valsad: Saurabh Gunavat, East Godavari: Sai Mithra.

A. Parikh, *Risks in Agriculture*, SpringerBriefs in Economics,
DOI 10.1007/978-981-10-6271-1_3

the risks faced by agriculturally developed nations with India's, we get to understand how much we might be lacking in resource provision or technology extension.

The following sections describe the trends in area and yields for each of the 18 crops in the sample districts. Cereals are taken up first, then pulses, then cash crops, and lastly horticultural crops are examined. Each case is examined with about 10 years' data. The arithmetic mean and the standard deviation is calculated for each variable. Volatility in production is calculated by looking at fluctuations around the mean—calculated as standard deviation/mean. This normalizes the standard deviation and makes it amenable for comparison.

Rate of increase or decrease for the decade is calculated using the semi-log regression: log (area) = $\alpha + \beta$ (year) or log (yield) = $\alpha + \beta$ (year). The β in such equations directly gives the growth rate for the whole period. This has been used only in the cases where there seems to be a distinct increasing or decreasing trend that needs to be confirmed. Otherwise measure for volatility is used because regression is not a good tool for highly volatile data.

3.2 Wheat

India is the second largest wheat producer in the world, next to China. India is followed by Russia, USA, and Canada (mapsofworld.com). From an importer of wheat in 1960s and 1970s, today India is an exporter of wheat, although most of its production is consumed domestically. The yields of main wheat producing states, Punjab and Haryana, are far higher (about 4740 kg/ha) than average yields of USA (around 3050 kg/ha) although lower than New Zealand (8100 kg/ha). Thus the northern states remain internationally competitive in wheat.

Our study concentrating mainly on semi-arid tropics looked at six districts for wheat: Ahmedabad, Junagadh, and Sabarkantha from Gujarat and Indore, Simla and Kanpur from rest of India. The districts differed in their yields. The following figures highlight the differences in yields among regions; the regional analysis follows in the next few sections.

District	Year	Yields (tonnes/ha)	Fluctuations around mean (past 10 years) (%)
Ahmedabad	2011–2012	2.50	19
Indore	2011–2012	4.92	40
Junagadh	2011–2012	3.84	15
Sabarkantha	2011–2012	2.61	8
Simla	2007–2008	1.99	12
Kanpur	2011–2012	3.46	12.9
India	2011–2012	3.18	12
New Zealand	2010	8.1	8
USA	2010–2011	3.08	7.1

3.2.1 Ahmedabad

The average wheat yields are low in Ahmedabad at 2.5 tonnes/ha. The yields between 2004–2005 and 2013–2014, however, have been increasing (Fig. 3.1). The regression equation with log (yields) = $a + b^*$ year gave an r^2 of 0.45; the t statistics was significant at 2.41 and it showed that the yields were increasing at the rate of 4.8% per annum.

There is too much variation in area cultivated. But there too, an increasing trend is noted.

3.2.2 Junagadh

The average yield of wheat in Junagadh between 1998–1999 and 2011–2012 (3.5 tonnes/ha) is slightly higher than that of India (2.78 tonnes/ha). However, fluctuations around the mean are around 15% for Junagadh (Fig. 3.2), 12% for Gujrat and 6% for India. Thus, the volatility is far more. The area under wheat fluctuates by almost 60% around the mean—it is extremely volatile. When we talked to the farmers, they told us that wheat is the rabi crop, grown after groundnut in kharif. If the rainfall has been deficient, they substitute coriander for wheat. Some farmers tried gram too. But when the rainfall is satisfactory, they all prefer wheat. Thus, the area volatility seems to be related to uncertainty of rains.

3.2.3 Sabarkantha

The average yield in Sabarkantha was 2.27 ton between 1998–1999 and 2011–2012, lower than the Indian average. Since 2003, the fluctuations in yields have

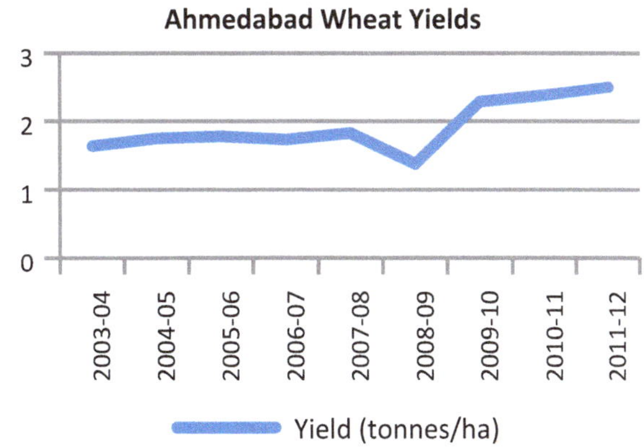

Fig. 3.1 Trends in the wheat yields of Ahmedabad. *Source* http://apy.dacnet.nic.in/crop_fryr_toyr.aspx

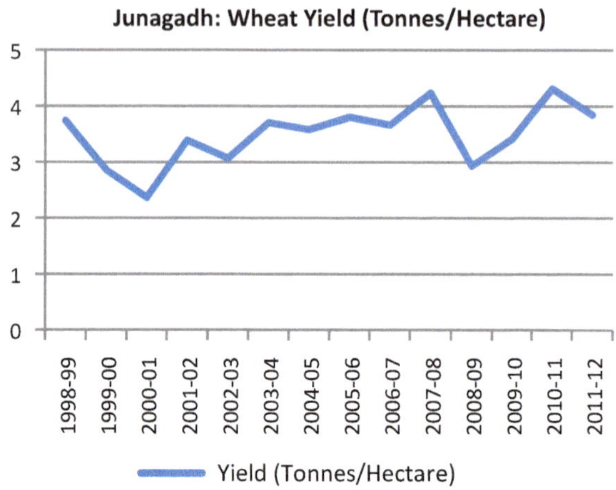

Fig. 3.2 Wheat yields in Junagadh. *Source* http://apy.dacnet.nic.in/crop_fryr_toyr.aspx

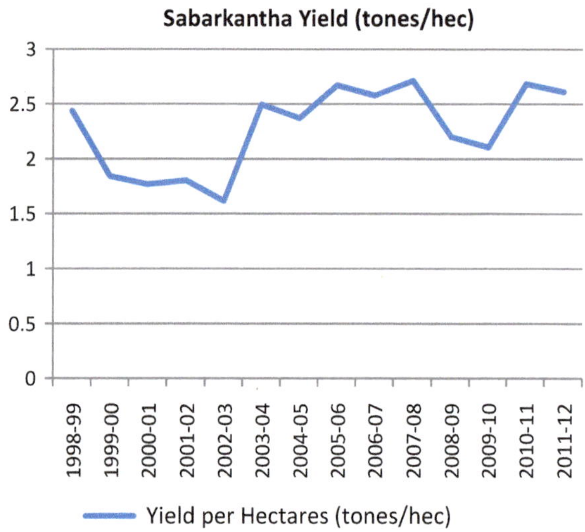

Fig. 3.3 Wheat yields in Sabarkantha. *Source* https://data.gov.in/catalog/district-wise-season-wise-crop-production-statistics

become lesser (Fig. 3.3)—8% around the mean—that is, lesser than the Indian average for the same period. We found from our survey that increase in irrigation facilities is making the yields steadier.

26 farmers from south Sabarkantha mentioned that they will always prefer growing wheat—This is because they eat wheat, and wheat also produces fodder for their cattle. Also the people who stopped growing maize around city area of Sabarkantha have started growing wheat instead. Thus, area under wheat is increasing since 2005. As mentioned in the previous paragraph, the increased means of irrigation also must have enabled more cultivation of wheat.

Thus, the three districts of Gujarat show very different trends—Ahmedabad has lower yields than Indian average but the yields have been slowly increasing;

Junagadh has better yield average but the fluctuation was higher compared to India and Sabarkantha has lower yields than Indian average but the yields have been stabilizing. The risks faced are the highest for the district with higher yields.

3.2.4 Indore

The yields were very high in Indore for the year 2012–2013 (4.92 tonne/ha—this level of productivity is comparable to Punjab) but the data showed wild fluctuations in yield (Fig. 3.4): the average yield from 1998–1999 to 2013–2014 was 2.79 tonnes per hectare and the standard deviation was high at 0.984—that means the yields fluctuate by 40% around the mean. Indore's average is comparable to Indian average (2.85 tonnes/ha) but the yield risk for India is just 12% around the mean—far lesser than Indore. There is a weak increasing trend in the wheat yields. It is hoped that the farmers would reach the same level of productivity and stability as the northern farmers but they need better access to irrigation. Madhya Pradesh is already competing with Punjab to take the first position as the highest producer of wheat.

27% of average land in Indore can be going in and out of cultivation per year. Also, the overall trend is showing a tendency to decline. The reason is not very clear as the prices and lagged area are only mildly correlated with $r = 0.38$. The explanation can be a lack of sufficient rains—Indore does not have much access to irrigation.

Fig. 3.4 Wheat yields in Indore. *Source* Ministry of Agriculture, Government of India (indiastat.com)

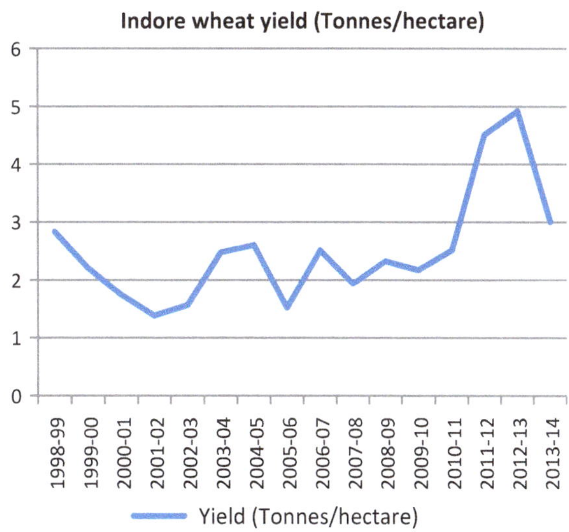

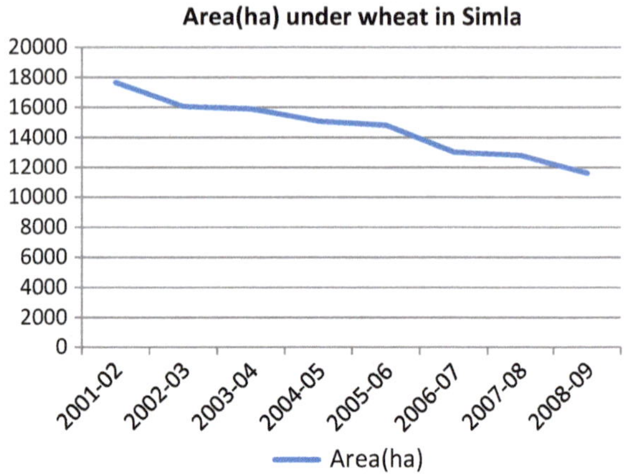

Fig. 3.5 Area under wheat in Simla. *Source* Directorate of Economics and Stastitics (http://apy.bacnet.nic.in/crop_fryr_toyr.aspx)

3.2.5 Simla

Area under wheat has been declining continuously for Simla (Fig. 3.5). Fewer and fewer people want to grow wheat. The reason might be the low yields. Simla produces 1.21 ton of wheat per hectare as against 2.49 ton of Indian average. The fluctuations around the mean was 12%—not very different from the national average. Thus, it seems that it is not so much the yield risk that is the problem in Simla but the low yields. A farmer explained this to us by saying that at higher altitudes, the yields are lesser.

As per the agricultural department, the production of maize and wheat is decreasing by 10–20% every year, as more and more farmers are growing vegetables because vegetables provide them with more income. In our sample of 17 wheat and maize farmers (they grow maize in the kharif and wheat in rabi), 9 farmers reported to have shifted to vegetable crops. Farmers also reported that they get hardly 1.19 ton/ha, as opposed to the average yields shown in the secondary data. Thus, vegetables prove to be better alternative for them.

Five farmers of Ghannati area (Simla) have an interesting story: They have started decreasing area under maize and wheat and the problem is monkeys. Monkeys from Shimla city were captured and transferred to this region. The monkeys have been a huge trouble as they destroy the crops. Farmers have tried everything they could (kept dogs, firing air guns, using real guns by firing them in the air, etc.) but nothing worked. At nights, the wild pigs ruin their crops. Helpless, they have stopped farming in their whole land, instead they farm only around their houses, as it is the region they can keep their eyes on and protect.

Harmish Sharma of Adyeog has one more reason to narrate: he was dependent on hired labors for the farming work, but the unskilled laborers ruined the cultivated area. Thus from the 30 bigha cultivable land, he is now left with 25 bigha.

Thus interestingly, we see varied preference for growing wheat: we see a strong declining trend in the area under wheat in Simla, slightly declining trend in Indore, a gradually increasing trend in all three Gujarat sample districts: Ahmedabad, Junagadh, and Sabarkantha.

3.2.6 *Kanpur*

The picture of wheat cultivation changes completely as we move to the Gangetic plains. Farmers prefer growing wheat on their lands: there are hardly any fluctuations in the area under wheat (5% around the mean). Yields (3.84 ton/ha) are higher than the national average (2.49 ton/ha), though they are lesser than Punjab and Haryana. Fluctuations in yields are also becoming lesser since last few years (Fig. 3.6). The riskiness and yields seem somewhat higher than India's but the difference is not statistically significant. Farmers here clearly have comparative advantage in growing wheat.

However when we compare the performance of our sample districts with international data, we realize that India has a long way to go. The yield per hectare is nine ton in New Zealand (faostat.fao.org), as opposed to just 2–3.5 ton in these districts. Also the fluctuation around the mean is never more than 8–9% for New Zealand or USA (faostat); it was more in all the districts under study except Sabarkantha. Thus, all the sample districts fare poorly on both the parameters.

In short, wheat farmers do suffer from the problem of low yields and yield fluctuations. Fortunately, price risk is almost non-existent—the prices in all the six districts show almost a smooth increasing trend. Wheat seems to be a safe crop to grow in that sense.

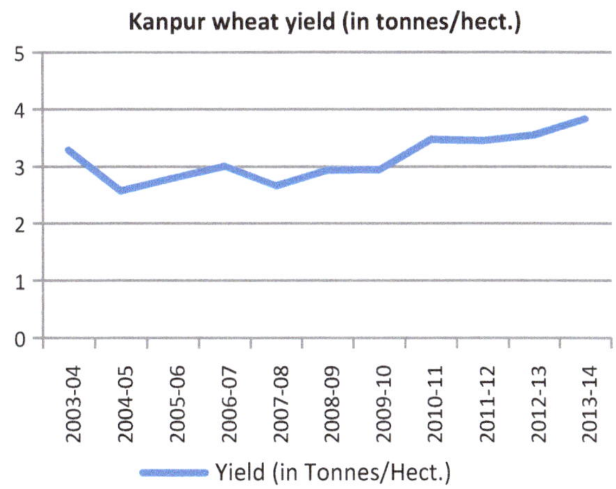

Fig. 3.6 Yields of wheat in Kanpur. *Source* Ministry of Agriculture, Government of India (indiastat.com)

3.3 Rice

India is the second largest producer of rice after China (mapsofworld.com). But average yields of India is only 3.16 ton which is much lesser than China's 6.39 ton/ha. Indonesia, Vietnam, and Thailand are the 3rd, 4th and 5th largest producers, respectively, but they all have better and more stable yields than India. It must be noted here that yields in Tamil Nadu are around 5 ton per hectare, which are comparable to developed nations. India has larger area under rice and hence is the second largest producer. The Indian cultivation technique and resource accessibility in many regions are poorer, making it lag in both yields and stability. The region-wise analysis is given in the following paragraphs.

Region	Year	Yield (ton/ha)	Fluctuations around mean (in last 10 years) (%)
Ahmedabad	2011–2012	2.75	14.7
Anand	2011–2012	2.23	10.3
E. Godavari	2011–2012	3.29	11.6
Goa	2011–2012	3.87	9.8
Kanpur	2011–2012	2.18	13.8
Surat	2011–2012	2.68	12.7
Valsad	2011–2012	2.2	10
India	2011–2012	3.59	9.85
China	2011	6.69	6.4

3.3.1 *Ahmedbad*

The rice cultivation in Ahmedabad seems to have gone through a full circle. The data shows that 2003–2004 onwards, yields were increasing and more and more hectares were brought under cultivation (Fig. 3.7). The yields started decreasing from 2006–2007 onwards (Fig. 3.8). As a result, from 2007–2008, the area under rice started declining. But the yields increased again in 2009–2010, and the yields were far more than the peak of past years. This seems to have made people go in a big way for rice again. Overall, fluctuations around mean are for yields is 15% but that seems to have changed the area under cultivation by 17% around the mean.

The average yields of the district (2.3 ton) between 2003–2004 and 2011–2012 are comparable with the national average of 2.2 ton/ha. However, the fluctuations around mean are much lesser for India: 9% compared to 15% for Ahmedabad. Wholesale prices have been rising every year, thus the risk of fall in prices does not seem to exist for rice.

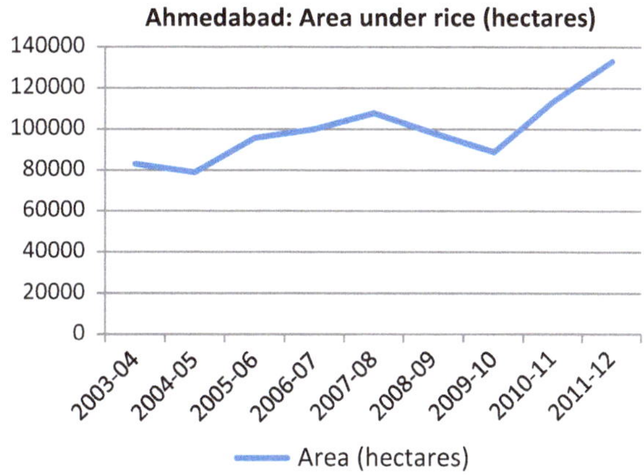

Fig. 3.7 Area under rice in Ahmedabad. *Source* http://apy.dacnet.nic.in/crop_fryr_toyr.aspx

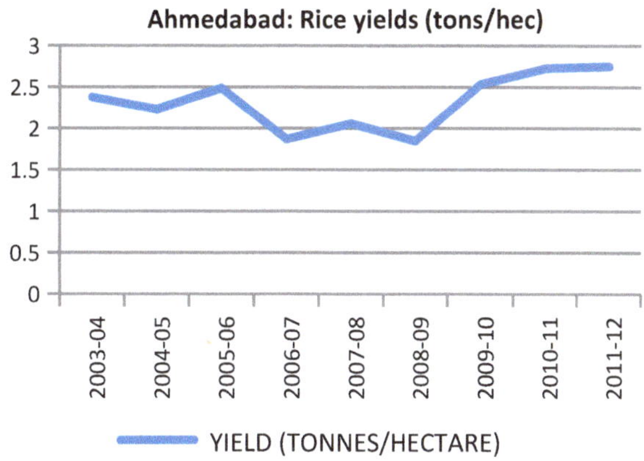

Fig. 3.8 Rice yields in Ahmedabad. *Source* http://apy.dacnet.nic.in/crop_fryr_toyr.aspx

3.3.2 Anand

The average yields of Anand (2.17 ton/ha) are slightly less than those of Ahmedabad (2.3 ton/ha) but the fluctuation around the mean is also lesser—10% compared to 15% in Ahmedabad. Thus, the yields are more stable in Anand (Fig. 3.9), although the risk is still more than the national average of 9%. Area under cultivation for rice has been fluctuating by only 8%, thus most farmers seem to be growing rice on a regular basis. Farmers from Boriyavi village explained why. They said that rice is staple food as well as a stable source of income hence it is never substituted for other crops. Also, farmers get MSP on rice which they do not get on growing fruits and vegetables so it is a relatively less risky proposition for them.

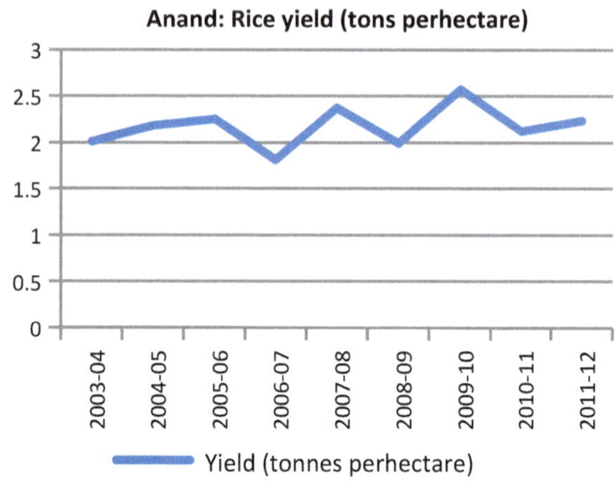

Fig. 3.9 Rice yields in Anand. *Source* http://apy.dacnet.nic.in/crop_fryr_toyr.aspx

3.3.3 East Godavari

In East Godavari, the area under cultivation has remained more or less the same for all years. The exceptions are years 2009–2010 and 2011–2012. Both these were drought years so people planted less of paddy. That is the reason why the fluctuation around the mean for area is only 8% (Fig. 3.10). Correlation between the price and area cultivated also is very low at 0.03, showing that the acreage under rice does not change with price. Our survey added some more insights: 10 farmers out of 14 seemed reluctant to adopt any change in their crops because they felt that they are best at growing rice and anything else would not bring better results. 3 farmers were interested in starting organic farming (not done yet) and one farmer is planning to grow flowers instead of rice. But all of these are still plans. The actual acreage continues to remain the same.

The rabi yields are considerably higher compared to the kharif yields. The overall average yields in East Godavari between 2004–2005 and 2014–2015 are 3

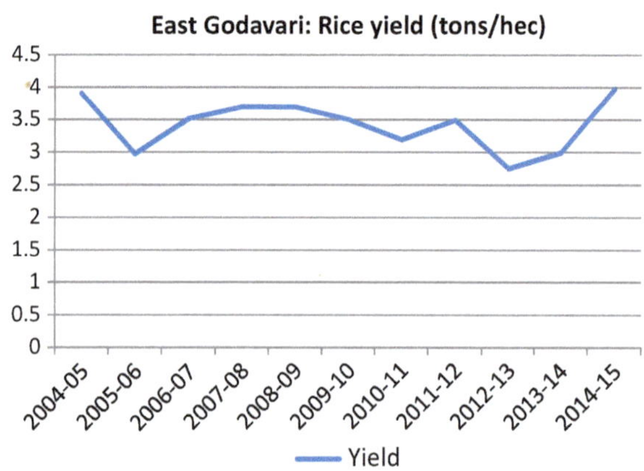

Fig. 3.10 Rice yields in East Godavari. *Source* http://apy.dacnet.nic.in/crop_fryr_toyr.aspx

ton/ha—comparable to the national average for the same period (3.16 ton/ha) but the average rabi yields are much higher at 5 ton/ha. This we found to be true for all districts. Rice is grown in kharif because it needs a lot of water but the weather is more conducive in winter. Therefore, regions that have a steady supply of irrigated water reap benefits of the winter weather by growing rice in rabi. That is maybe the reason why China's average yields are 6.4 ton/ha—China's rice plains are cooler than India's at any given time.

East Godavari's performance seems to be comparable to the national in almost all parameters. The yield fluctuations in East Godavari are 11% around the mean. This is very close to the national average of 9%. But yield fluctuations are much more volatile than China's (3.3%).

3.3.4 Goa

In Goa, almost 8000 hectares went out of paddy cultivation in 2001–2002. The state hit a peak in 1998–1999 at 55,534 hectares but by 2011–2012, it dropped to 47,237 hectares. The area cultivated now fluctuates in this lower range only (Fig. 3.11). However, the decision to put the area under rice does not seem to depend too much on price since the correlation between the area and price is 0.116. Some other factors seem to be at work—The 19 farmers who we interviewed felt that this must be mainly because of the switch to horticultural crops. Loss of land to tourism and mining can be other explanations. A farmer who works in cashew processing factory confessed that he has no time to look after crops—he gave up rice cultivation in 2008.

The average yields of Goa (3.87 ton) are higher than the national average (3.16 ton). The fluctuation around the mean (9%) is the same as the national average (9%) (Fig. 3.12). Thus, the overall performance of Goa rice is better than the national. Goa does better than the major rice producing states of India: Chhatisgarh (1.59 ton), Bihar (2.158 ton), West Bengal (2.7 ton) and Uttar Pradesh (2.38 ton). We feel

Fig. 3.11 Area under rice in Goa. *Source* www.agri.goa.gov.in/uploads/

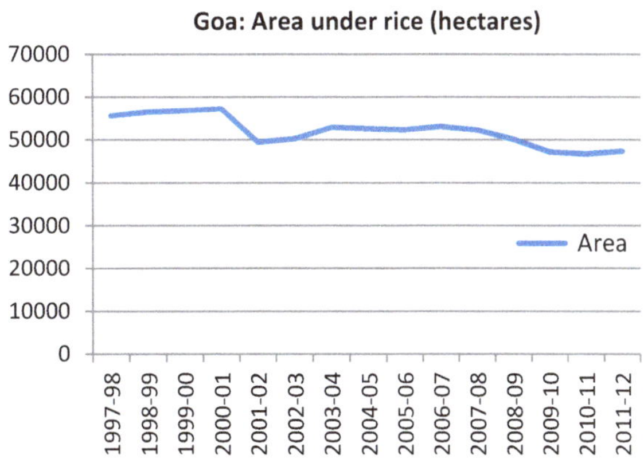

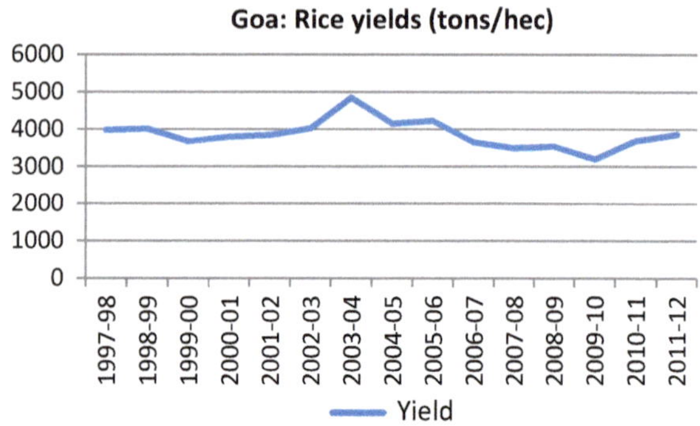

Fig. 3.12 Rice yields in Goa. *Source* www.agri.goa.gov.in/uploads/

that the main reason for this must be a better educational level of the farmers and hence better adoption of the technology. However, we see a slight declining trend in yields of late. It might be because of reduced interest, as discussed above; we are not too sure of the reason.

3.3.5 *Kanpur*

Kanpur grows wheat in rabi. The same land is used to grow rice in the monsoon. The land under rice is gradually declining though. The variations around mean are 10% but the general direction is toward decline (Fig. 3.13). In our field survey, 47 out of 72 farmers explained that lesser rainfall and generally uncertain monsoon in the recent years were the main reasons affecting the acreage under rice. Interestingly, 60 farmers said that poor electricity supply for running the irrigation pumps is a major problem. They have to shift to the rented costlier diesel pumps that increase the cost of production.

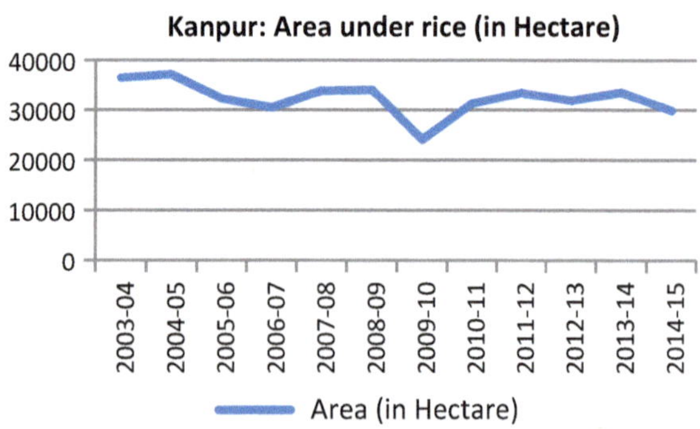

Fig. 3.13 Area under rice in Kanpur. *Source* Ministry of Agriculture, Government of India (Indiastat.com)

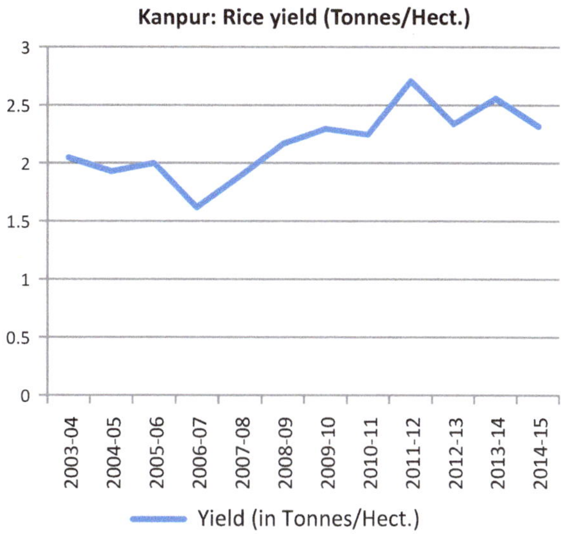

Fig. 3.14 Rice yields in Kanpur. *Source* Ministry of Agriculture, Government of India (indiastat.com)

The yields in Kanpur show gradual increasing trend (Fig. 3.14). However, average yields (2.17 ton) are lower compared to the national average (3.16 ton). The fluctuations (13%) are somewhat higher than the national average (9%). In short, the natural advantage that Kanpur has for wheat is not there for rice.

3.3.6 Surat

The average yields of Surat (2.075 ton/ha) are lower than all the other districts seen till now. The yields are increasing (Fig. 3.16), but they are slightly lower than other districts of Gujarat, let alone India (3.16 ton/ha). The fluctuations (12.7%) include the increasing trend also, thus the overall fluctuations are lesser. Risk might not be too high in growing rice (Fig. 3.15).

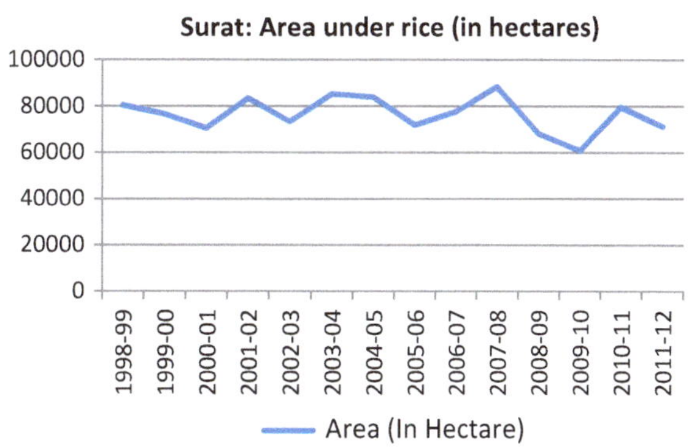

Fig. 3.15 Area under rice in Surat. *Source* http://apy.dacnet.nic.in/crop_fryr_toyr.aspx

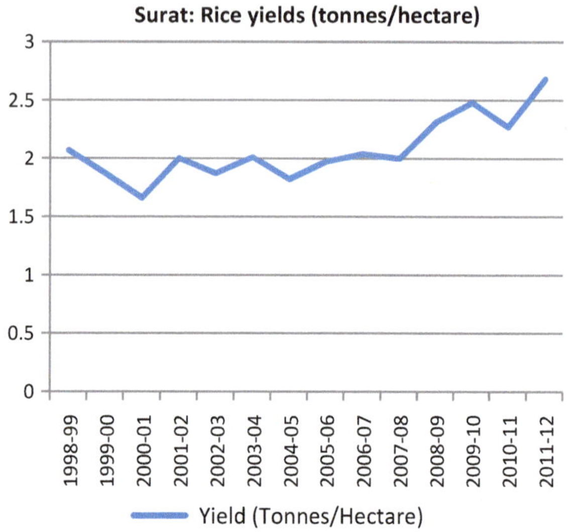

Fig. 3.16 Rice yields in Surat. *Source* http://apy.dacnet.nic.in/crop_fryr_toyr.aspx

The area under rice fluctuates around the mean by about 10%—thus it seems to be generally grown as a regular crop (Fig. 3.15). However, a slight downward movement is noticed in the trend—it is statistically insignificant at present but it seems to be moving that way. Farmers might be shifting to other crops slowly. Our survey was able to throw some light on this. Most surveyed farmers in Surat take two crops of rice but farmers having the problem of reliable water supply have started cultivating til and wheat in the rabi season instead of rice because these crops need less water. 5 farmers out of 45 (11.11%) have substituted rice with til and wheat. As discussed above, this is not a statistically significant number, but the change seems to be taking place. There is no change or substitution of rice in kharif as all farmers grow rice in this season.

3.3.7 Valsad

Valsad farmers used to devote a lot of acreage under rice before 2003–2004 but after that, the acreage declined almost by half (Fig. 3.17). The acreage started gradually increasing but it has still not reached the levels of 2003–2004. The farmers in Umarsadi confirmed this trend saying that initially they used to grow rice on average on 4–5 acres but now they have reduced the acreage to only so much that could provide for their home consumption. The reasons are three-fold: lack of labor, decrease in rainfall and animal menace. They are substituting rice with sugarcane and mango as there is less effort in growing those and are more profitable.

The yields do not fluctuate very wildly around the mean (Fig. 3.18). The risk is 10%, which is comparable to the national average. Hence, it could be called a safe

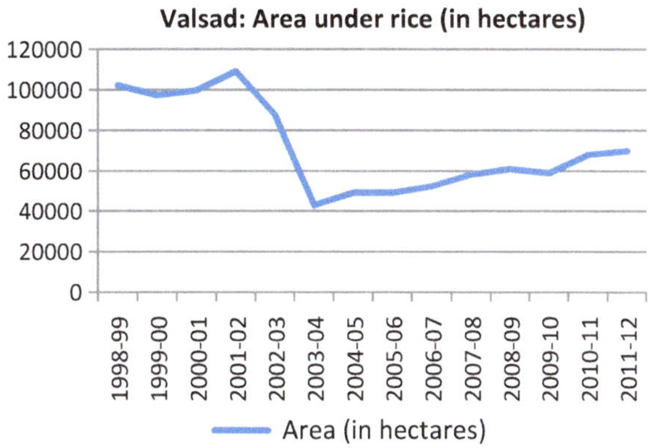

Fig. 3.17 Area under rice in Valsad. *Source* http://apy.dacnet.nic.in/crop_fryr_toyr.aspx

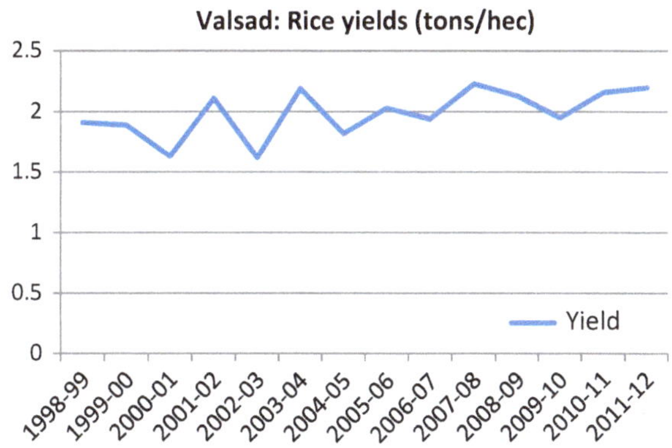

Fig. 3.18 Rice yields in Valsad. *Source* http://apy.dacnet.nic.in/crop_fryr_toyr.aspx

crop for farmers in Valsad. But the average yields (1980 kg/ha) are lowest among all districts and far lower than the national average (3160 kg/ha).

3.3.8 Conclusion

The average rice yields in India are around 3 ton/ha. It falls far short of the international average yield of China (6.4 ton), Australia (10.1 ton), USA (7.5 ton) and Russia (5.2 ton). China's yield risk is only 3% whereas India's is 9% and as we saw, most districts studied by us had higher yield risk than the national average. The reason, as our analysis above shows, mainly lies in accessibility to water.

It should be mentioned here that the district averages also can conceal a large range of yields—we found in Anand that the yield for rice, tobacco, and bajra was found to be 5.6, 3.75, 4.3 ton/ha from the field surveys as opposed to average yield of 2.17, 1.89, 1.87 ton/ha from secondary data. The reason could be that our survey was conducted in villages that were known for growing these crops. Other villages might be far behind in technology adoption or resource accessibility.

The fluctuations in yield are slightly higher for wheat compared to rice at the national level. Thus rice is less risky. And still, there is a noticeable difference between wheat and rice acreage: 4 out of 5 study districts had wide fluctuations in wheat acreage but the there was no definite declining trend, except in Simla. Farmers seem to be attracted back toward wheat, whenever the conditions become favorable. As opposed to that, we found a declining trend in acreage for rice in four out of seven districts. Farmers seem to be taking up production of some other crops in these areas and are shifting away from rice.

3.4 Bajra

A staple food for the poor in many regions of India, bajra is grown widely. It is a crop that grows in dry and arid regions, does not require much water or soil fertility and can withstand extreme heat. Thus, it is suitable for the semi-arid tropics in India. We have studied three regions for bajra; the results are given in the following paragraphs.

Region	Avg yield (ton/ha)	Fluctuations around mean (%)
Jodhpur	584.44	55.52
Anand	1878	13
Kanpur	1574	19
Rajasthan	600.61	40
India	872.13	20
USA (millet)	1458	26

3.4.1 Jodhpur

There was a severe drought in the year 2002–2003. Most farmers could not grow anything or the crop just dried up. The yield does not show this effect much because it shows the yields from the few fields that could cultivate with irrigation that year (Fig. 3.19). The acreage declined (Fig. 3.20) from 652,067 to 45,060 ha (dropped by 93%). Thus droughts can completely destroy crops and agriculture economy in Jodhpur. Here is one district that would desperately need help in the times of drought.

The average bajra yields of Jodhpur (584.44 kg/ha) are far lesser than the national average of Bajra (872.13 kg/ha) but it is close to the state average of 600.61 kg/ha of Rajasthan. The yields fluctuate widely around the mean—to the

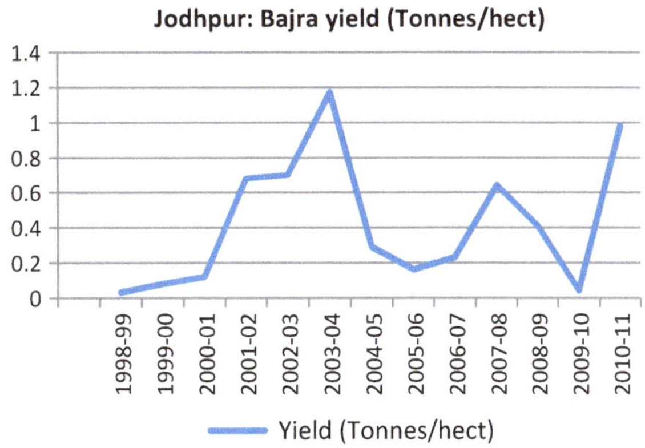

Fig. 3.19 Bajra yields in Jodhpur. *Source* Directorate of economics and statistics, Government of Rajasthan (indiastat.com)

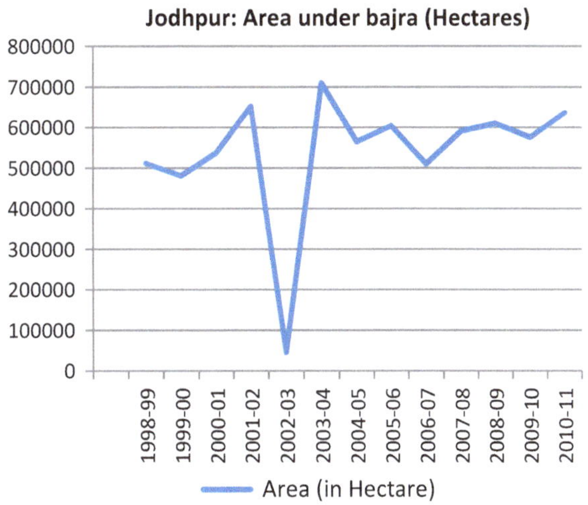

Fig. 3.20 Area under bajra in Jodhpur. *Source* Directorate of economics and statistics, Government of Rajasthan (indiastat.com)

extent of 55.52%. The Rajasthan yields also fluctuate greatly—40% around the mean. This is extremely high volatility and remains an area of concern. Compared to this, the fluctuations are lower for India—20% around the mean. Taken by itself, 20% also seems like a high level of fluctuations (rice and wheat are far more stable, as the previous sections showed), but considering that the even USA has the volatility of 26% in its yields of millets, it looks like a risky crop all over the world.

We could not find exact data on pearl millet (bajra) for international comparison. However, we found that the USA grows millet, that is the same family of crops. The yields of millets in the USA are 1458 kg/ha—2.5 times the yields of Jodhpur.

The area under bajra fluctuated by 11% around the mean between 1998–1999 and 2010–2011 (the outlier year of 2002–2003 is excluded from this calculation). This is higher than the national average of 6.7%. When we talked to the farmers in Jodhpur, we were told that the farmers rotate 4–5 crops—different pieces of land are used for the crops to ensure that the same crop is not grown on the same piece. They feel this practice ensure better soil fertility. This rotation practices might have affected the actual calculation of land. Otherwise, farmers say that they grow bajra regularly.

Since 2003–2004, there is mainly increasing trend in prices of bajra. Thus the farmer faces the yield risk but price risk is not significant.

3.4.2 Anand

Bajra cultivation shows a very interesting trend in Anand. People were putting lesser area under bajra till 2008–2009 (Fig. 3.21). The bajra yields were declining gradually during this period (Fig. 3.22). However, the area under cultivation and yields both suddenly increase in 2009–2010. After that, both the yields and area under bajra have been increasing.

Our field survey could not explain this trend much. A group of marginal farmers from Boriyavi (Anand district) told us that bajra was consumed by them every day; therefore, it is produced by all marginal farmers. At times, it can be substituted with jowar. In Chikhodra, only small part of the land is devoted to bajra. Thus, the changing acreage must have happened in some other villages that we could not visit.

The average yields of Bajra in Anand of 1878 kg/ha are far higher compared to the national yield of 872.1 kg/ha. The yields are higher than millet yield of USA also! The fluctuations around the mean are also higher for the USA—26% as opposed to just 13% in Anand. Anand seems to have a strong comparative advantage in growing Bajra.

Our data shows a good correlation between rainfall and yields—$r = 0.6$—maybe bajra is grown more when rains were good.

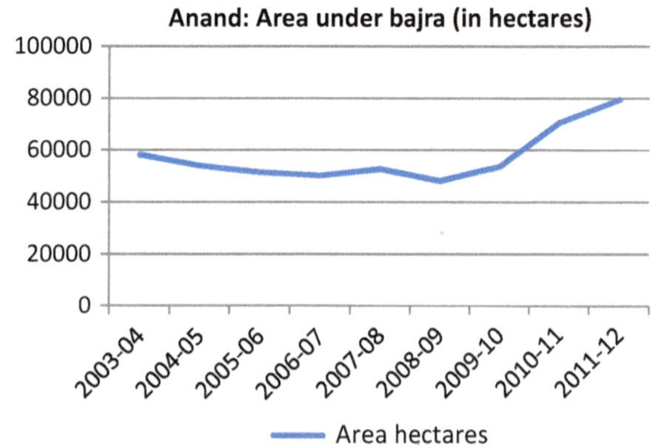

Fig. 3.21 Area under Bajra in Anand. *Source* http://apy.dacnet.nic.in/crop_fryr_toyr.aspx

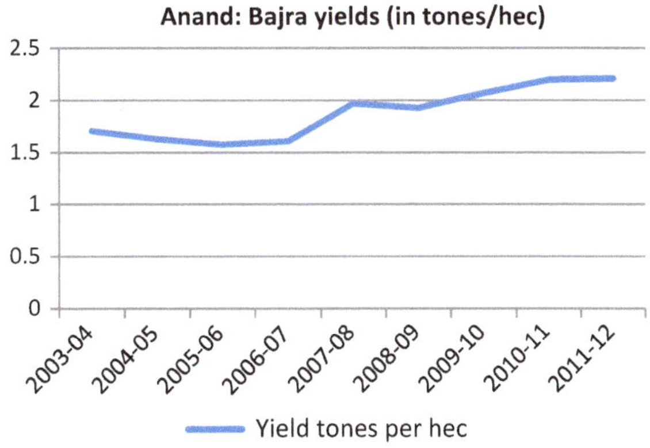

Fig. 3.22 Yields of Bajra in Anand. *Source* http://apy.dacnet.nic.in/crop_fryr_toyr.aspx

3.4.3 *Kanpur*

The yields of Kanpur (1574 kg/ha) are higher than the national average although a little lesser than Anand. The fluctuations in yields (19%) are also higher (Fig. 3.23) compared to Anand but far lower than Jodhpur, or even the USA.

Still, farmers in Kanpur do not seem to consider Bajra as an important crop. There are wide fluctuations in the area under bajra (Fig. 3.24). The fluctuations are as high as 63% around the mean. The r between rainfall and yield is insignificant at 0.335. Thus, the weather might not be an important factor in deciding to cultivate bajra. The correlation between area and price was significant at 0.68. Thus, bajra prices might be making a difference in the acreage. Our field survey was limited for this region, so we could not get much insights from the survey.

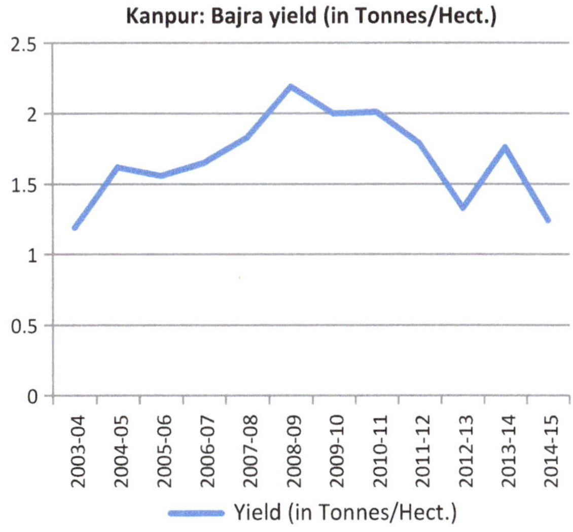

Fig. 3.23 Bajra yields in Kanpur. *Source* Ministry of Agriculture, Government of India (indiastat.com)

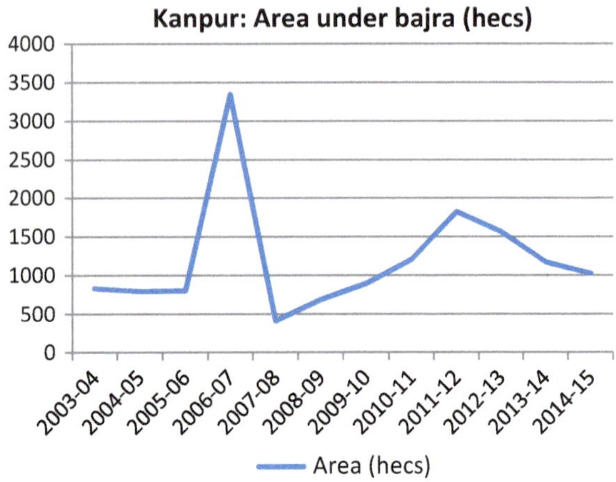

Fig. 3.24 Area under Bajra in Kanpur. *Source* Ministry of Agriculture, Government of India (indiastat.com)

3.4.4 Conclusion

Bajra represents an interesting trend because the acreage has been almost constant in Jodhpur, slightly increasing in Anand and widely fluctuating in Kanpur. In western India, it is a staple crop hence its acreage cannot decline too much. It is considered as a nutritious coarse cereal. It is good to know that some regions of India have high comparative advantage in growing this crop.

3.5 Maize

Maize is an important cereal crop. It is a staple food for tribal populations in many regions of Gujarat. In many other places also, maize is used as both food and fodder. Only two districts were growing maize from our sample. Their trends are described in the next section.

Region	Yield (ton/ha)	Fluctuations around mean (in last 10 years) (%)
Sabarkantha	1.44	32.3
Simla	2.22	21.4
India	2.07	14
USA	5.27	8

3.5.1 Sabarkantha

Area under maize shows a constant declining trend after 2003–2004—it decreased from 146.3 thousand hectares in 2003–2004 to 94 thousand hectares in 2010–2011. The reason cannot be price because prices are rising constantly (see Table 3.1).

25 Farmers of the northeast area from Juna Chamu and Kothan (both Vadali tehsil) village insisted that there is no decrease in cultivation area under maize. They claim that maize production has increased. They say that there is no question for growing anything else in place of maize because maize is the staple food for the people of north east Sabarkantha. They get their cattle feed also from maize.

We suspect that the decline must have happened in more developed areas of Sabarkantha where the staple food is wheat and not maize. We were told by the villagers there that when fields are closer to the city areas in Sabarkantha, they have started substituting wheat for maize.

The yields are very volatile: the fluctuation around mean is 32%. The average yields are 1.44 ton/ha which is far lesser than the national average of 2.07 ton/ha. The volatility is lower for India at 14% around the mean and even lower for the USA at 8% around the mean. The main maize growing regions of Sabarkantha are in northeast, the area that is considered agriculturally backward. That must explain such low yields.

In general, the yields of all three crops under study are lower for Sabarkantha. Water does not seem to be the issue since everyone (except in the northeast region)

Table 3.1 Area, production and yield of maize in Sabarkantha district

Year	Area (ha)	Production (ton)	Production per hectares (P/A)
1998–1999	122,100	243,600	1.99
1999–2000	117,700	178,300	1.51
2000–2001	108,800	93,600	0.86
2001–2002	132,400	284,100	2.14
2002–2003	143,700	181,000	1.25
2003–2004	146,300	266,700	1.82
2004–2005	127,300	143,500	1.12
2005–2006	125,400	245,800	1.96
2006–2007	115,700	68,200	0.58
2007–2008	101,100	146,400	1.44
2008–2009	90,300	130,900	1.44
2009–2010	88,300	90,700	1.02
2010–2011	94,200	154,600	1.64
Average	116407.6923	171338.4615	1.44
Std Dev	19116.50515	70245.2672	0.468
Risk	0.1642202914	0.4099795607	0.323

https://data.gov.in/catalog/district-wise-season-wise-crop-production-statistics

Table 3.2 Farm harvest price of maize in Sabarkantha

1998	541
1999	559
2000	516
2001	490
2002	626
2003	515
2004	521
2005	608
2006	729
2007	702
2008	756
2009	956
2010	1067

http://www.indiastat.com/agriculture/2/agriculturalprices/6527/farmharvestprices/31705/stats.aspx

seems to have some access to irrigated water. The knowledge of technology seems to be wanting in this region.

The price risk, as shown in Table 3.2, has been very less. Prices are mostly increasing, especially since 2005.

3.5.2 Simla

Just like Sabarkantha, area under cultivation of maize is gradually declining—at the rate of about 9% p.a., as shown by the semi-log regression.

The yields are 2.22 ton/ha which is comparable to the national average (2.07 ton/ha) although far lower than USA's 5.273 ton/ha. The yield fluctuations around the mean are high at 21%, these are much higher than 14% for India and 8% for the USA.

The technology of growing corn has advanced a lot in last few decades. It is disturbing to know that our sample farmers have not been able to master this technology.

3.6 Jowar

Just like bajra, jowar also is a suitable crop for semi-arid tropics and hence is popular in India as both foodgrain and as animal feed. Jowar is used in some industries also like ethanol and paper making. In our sample, just one district—Surat—was growing jowar.

Surat	1500	12.25%
Gujart	950	19.06%
India	850	10.6%
USA	4330	12.79%
Mexico	3710	9.74%

3.6.1 *Surat*

Area under jowar is on the decline in Surat (Table 3.3). The semi-log regression shows that the area is declining at the rate of 5% p.a. during the study period. Jowar seems to be a less preferred crop now in Surat. The yields seem to have stagnated over the period of time—this could be because farmers are investing lesser on this crop compared to others.

	Surat	Gujarat	India	USA	Mexico
Yield risk (%)	12.25	19.06	10.6	12.79	9.74
Ave. yield (ton/ha)	1.3	0.95	0.85	4.33	3.71

However, the actual yields are high in Surat. The average yields of jowar in Gujarat (950 kg/ha) are higher than the national average (850 kg/ha). The yields in Surat are higher at 1500 kg/ha. Surat is agriculturally developed region in Gujarat. Therefore, it does not come as a surprise that the farmers get better yields than

Table 3.3 Area, production and yield for jowar, Surat district

Year	Area (ha)	Production (ton)	Yield (ton/ha)
1998–1999	29,800	41,200	1.38
1999–2000	37,600	63,400	1.69
2000–2001	34,000	38,300	1.13
2001–2002	55,200	63,000	1.14
2002–2003	31,500	45,900	1.46
2003–2004	45,500	59,800	1.31
2004–2005	36,300	51,500	1.42
2005–2006	32,900	44,400	1.35
2006–2007	31,600	38,300	1.21
2007–2008	40,500	56,300	1.39
2008–2009	18,700	22,100	1.18
2009–2010	28,700	38,000	1.32
2010–2011	18,700	22,100	1.18
2011–2012	18,200	20,400	1.12

Source http://apy.dacnet.nic.in/crop_fryr_toyr.aspx

average. However, if we compare this to USA (4330 kg/ha) or Mexico (3710 kg/ha), our productivity turns out to be extremely low. The local maxima cannot match the global maxima.

The Surat yields are somewhat more volatile (12.25%) than India's (10.6%) but less than Gujarat's (19.06%); they are comparable to the USA fluctuations (12.79%).

The farm harvest prices are consistently rising for jowar (gujstat.com). Thus, price risk does not seem to be very high for the farmers.

In fine, Surat seems to be well suited for growing jowar. It gets good yields, and has stable production trends. Still, the area under jowar is declining. Farmers told us during our field survey that their first preferences are rice and sugarcane. Jowar is a subsidiary crop. It must be declining in importance because of that.

3.7 Pulses

Pulses are an important part of the diet in India—the main source of protein—usually eaten with cereals to make a whole meal. Indian meals are not complete without pulses. India grows many varieties of pulses—we have taken four pulses here: moong, moth, urad, and chana. India is a largest consumer and producer of chana. We found that among all pulses under the study, it was chana that was doing well. The problems faced by each of these pulses are looked at in the next section.

Region	Average yield (ton/ha)	Fluctuations around mean (in last 10 years) (%)
Moong		
Jodhpur	232	57.3
Rajasthan	695	21.09
E. Godavari	270	36
India (gram)	829	6.55
Canada (gram)	1765	14.09
Moth		
Jodhpur	242.5	56.3
Rajasthan	402	34
Urad		
Valsad	510	31
E. Godavari	490	47.8
Chana		
Indore	930	23
India	834	7
USA	1540	6

3.7.1 Jodhpur: Moong

As Fig. 3.25 shows, except for the last year (which is an estimate and they are usually unreliable), the overall trend in yields shows stagnancy. Pulses have not benefited much by advances in agriculture technology in India hence the stagnancy does not come as a surprise. The average yields are stagnant for India and Rajasthan also.

The average yields of Jodhpur (232 kg/ha) are almost one-third of the yields in Rajasthan (695 kg/ha). The average yields are 829 kg/ha for India.

The Jodhpur farmers are totally dependent on rains. Hence it is no wonder that the correlation between the rainfall and yield is 0.64.

The fluctuations in yields around the mean are as high as 57.3% for Jodhpur (the year 2009–2010 is not counted as nothing was grown in that year). This is much higher than the risks faced by the Rajasthan farmers—21.09% around the mean. We could not find data for moong (green gram) for India but we found the gram data. The volatility in yields for gram in India (6.85%) is interestingly far lesser than all of these and is actually almost comparable to the cereals. Figures 3.25 and 3.26 show the stark contrast between Jodhpur and India.

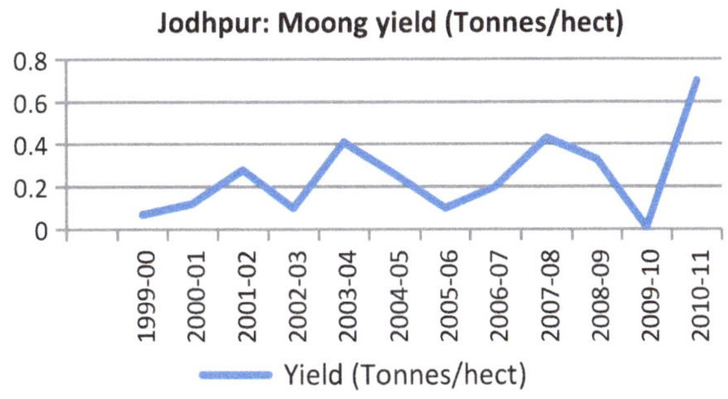

Fig. 3.25 Moong Yields in Jodhpur. *Source* Directorate of economics and statistics, Government of Rajasthan (indiastat.com)

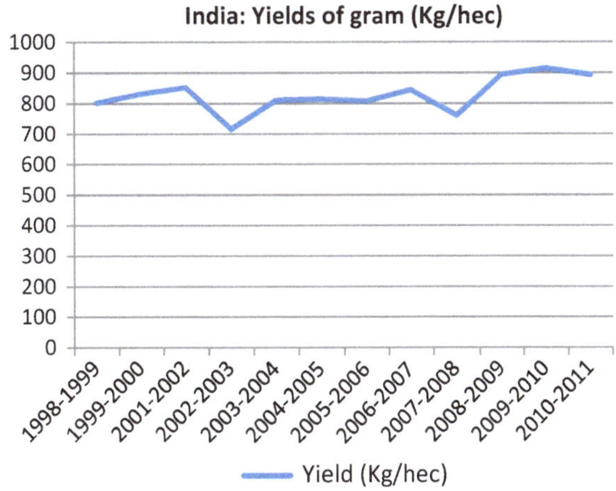

Fig. 3.26 Variations in yields of gram for India. *Source* Ministry of Agriculture, Government of India (indiastat.com)

We have used the gram data for international comparison also because data on green gram was not available. The leading producer in the world for gram is Canada. The gram yields are double compared to India at 1765 kg/ha. The Canadian yields are almost 6 times more than Jodhpur. This shows a dire need to improve the resource accessibility in Jodhpur.

The volatility in yields is more in Canada (14.9%) compared to India (6.85%). But even at its lowest point of the yields curve, Canada gets higher yield than India. Thus, lesser volatility cannot be considered as an advantage for India.

2008 onwards the gram prices increased sharply. Thus, price risk does not seem to be as much a worry for moong farmers as the volatility in yields.

3.7.2 East Godavari: Moong

The average yields of East Godavari are almost the same as Jodhpur: they are very low at 270 kg/ha. The yields increased slightly in 2012–2013, but are still much lower than the national average (829 kg/ha).

The yields are showing an increasing trend from 2011–2012 but the fluctuations in yields are very high (Fig. 3.27) at 36% around the mean. This is lesser than Jodhpur but more than Canada (14.9%) and India (6.85%).

The area under moong has been constantly declining over last 10 years (Fig. 3.28). At the same time, the prices have been consistently rising. Our data analysis shows that the percentage increase in prices are just not enough to cover the percentage loss in production when yields drop. Because of this, the overall incomes of the farmers decline drastically when production is less. The yield volatility seems to have made the farmers weary of moong production. There is no logical contradiction in the farmers' decision making.

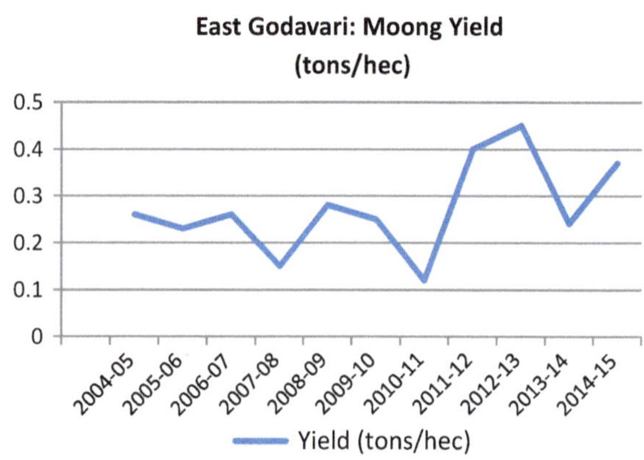

Fig. 3.27 Yields of moong in East Godavari. *Source* http://apy.dacnet.nic.in/crop_fryr_toyr.aspx

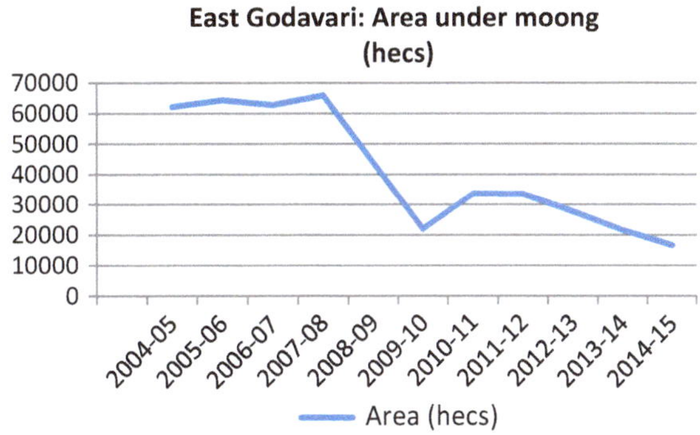

Fig. 3.28 Area under moong in East Godavari. *Source* apy.dacnet.nic.in/crop_fryr_toyr.aspx

3.7.3 *Jodhpur: Moth*

Area under moth has been fluctuating greatly but the general trend seems to be stagnant. Yields are also stagnant (Fig. 3.29). The average yields are 242.5 kg/ha in Jodhpur which compares very poorly with 402 kg/ha of Rajasthan and 614.61 kg/ha of India (the Indian figure includes all pulses). The Canadian yields (1765 kg/ha), as pointed out before, are far higher than any of these.

Fluctuations around the mean are similar to moong: 56.30%. The production fluctuates very wildly in Jodhpur. This is far higher than the state, national or international average, as discussed before. The correlation with rainfall is significant (0.655) thus rainfall seems to be a major factor causing such fluctuations. The data from Jodhpur clearly shows the miserable condition that the farmers have to live in.

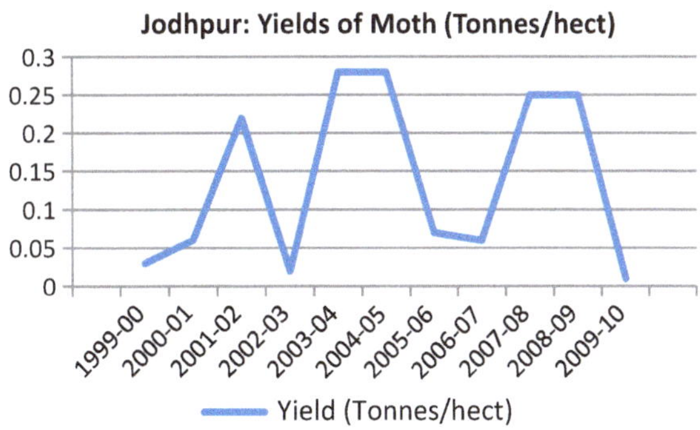

Fig. 3.29 Yields of moth in Jodhpur. *Source* Directorate of economics and statistics, Government of Rajasthan (indiastat.com)

Table 3.4 Area, production and yield of urad in Valsad

Year	Area	Production	Yield
1998–1999	6000	1000	0.17
1999–2000	6400	1500	0.23
2000–2001	5700	1600	0.28
2001–2002	7400	4200	0.57
2002–2003	6800	3900	0.57
2003–2004	4500	3000	0.67
2004–2005	5900	3800	0.64
2005–2006	5900	3500	0.59
2006–2007	5300	3200	0.6
2007–2008	5400	3100	0.57
2008–2009	5300	3200	0.6
2009–2010	5400	2700	0.5
2010–2011	5900	3200	0.54
2011–2012	5800	3600	0.62

Source http://apy.dacnet.nic.in/crop_fryr_toyr.aspx

3.7.4 Valsad: Urad

Area under urad is more or less constant (Table 3.4). People use it mainly for home consumption. The yields increased till 2001–2002 but have stagnated since then. The average yields of 510 kg/ha are surely far higher than Jodhpur but lower than the national average of pulse yields of 620 kg/ha. And the international comparison is as poor as all other districts. Fluctuation around mean is 31% (Fig. 3.30), which is slightly higher than Indore but lower than Jodhpur. None of the pulses under consideration seem to be giving either promising yields or riskless production.

3.7.5 East Godavari: Urad

The yields of urad had stagnated in East Godavari till 2012–2013 to around 200 kg/ha but there is considerable increase in yields since then (Table 3.5). The yields were 490 kg/ha in 2014–2015. They still fall much short of the national average of 820 kg/ha and Canada's yield of 1760. The yield fluctuations are very high at 47.8% around the mean. Rainfall cannot be the influencing factor because the correlation of yields with rainfall is weak at 0.43.

The urad prices are showing a strong increasing trend. But the area under urad is showing a declining trend (Fig. 3.31). We suspect that the yield risk must be a responsible factor for this, as explained under the section on moong in East Godavari.

3.7.6 Indore: Chana

Indore is a major producer of chick pea (Chana). Madhya Pradesh contributes about 30–35% of the country's production of chick pea.

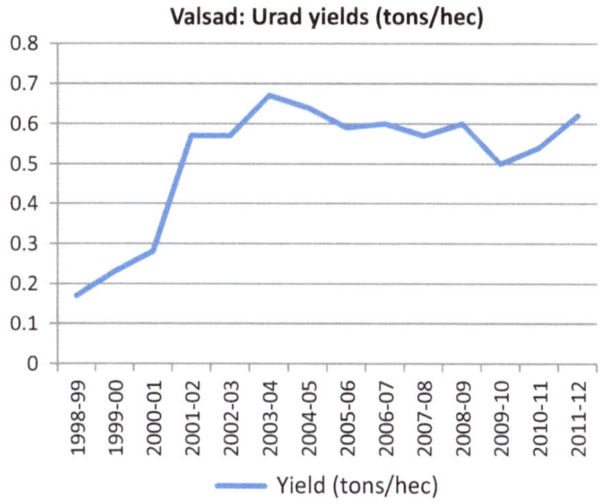

Fig. 3.30 Yields of urad in Valsad. *Source* http://apy.dacnet.nic.in/crop_fryr_toyr.aspx

Table 3.5 Area, production and yield of urad in East Godavari

Year	Season	Urad		
		Area	Production	Yield
2004–2005	Kharif	421	203	0.48
	Rabi	44,482	11,165	0.25
	Total	44,903	11,368	0.25
2005–2006	Kharif	1442	496	0.34
	Rabi	44,862	8210	0.18
	Total	46,304	8706	0.19
2006–2007	Kharif	1034	396	0.38
	Rabi	48,368	12,624	0.26
	Total	49,402	13,020	0.26
2007–2008	Rabi	48,000	10,000	0.21
	Total	48,000	10,000	0.2
2008–2009	Kharif	995	361	0.36
	Rabi	31,934	8526	0.27
	Total	32,929	8887	0.27
2009–2010	Kharif	4001	1180	0.29
	Rabi	32,258	1419	0.04
	Total	36,259	2599	0.07
2010–2011	Kharif	1422	600	0.42
	Rabi	21,387	4470	0.21
	Total	22,809	5070	0.22

(continued)

Table 3.5 (continued)

Year	Season	Urad		
		Area	Production	Yield
2011–2012	Kharif	3330	1668	0.5
	Rabi	27,849	2674	0.1
	Total	31,179	4342	0.14
2012–2013	Kharif	1298	919	0.71
	Rabi	20,768	7606	0.37
	Total	22,066	8525	0.39
2013–2014	Kharif	1969	1231	0.63
	Rabi	18,625	2403	0.13
	Total	20,594	3634	0.18
2014–2015	Kharif	2605	2670	1.02
	Rabi	18,500	7641	0.41
	Total	21,105	10,311	0.49

Source http://apy.dacnet.nic.in/crop_fryr_toyr.aspx

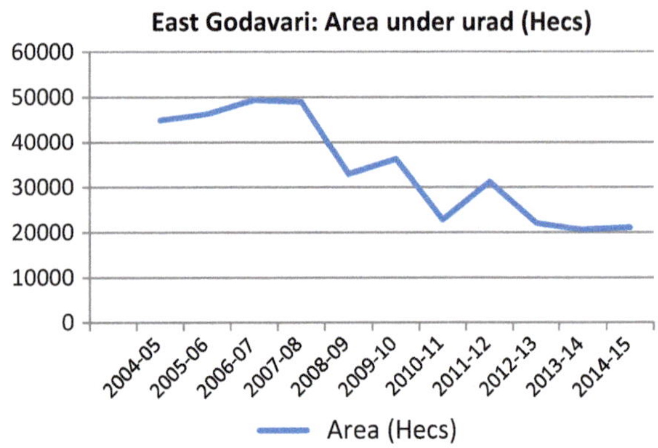

Fig. 3.31 Area under urad for East Godavari. *Source* http://apy.dacnet.nic.in/crop_fryr_toyr.aspx

Area under chana in Indore was stagnant till 2008–2009. Then it sharply increased then again decreased but the decrease is not as sharp as the increase (Fig. 3.32). The farmers of Jamli explained why this might happen: Chana is grown only on a part of the land, the rest is used for potatoes and onions (they are more profitable). Depending on the weather, acreage for potatoes/onions gets decided. On the remaining land, chana is grown. Chana does not need much water so it could be grown even when the rains are lesser (that is why the correlation between acreage and rain is low at 0.2). That is how the acreage fluctuates—but since chana is always grown on some part, it never declines too much.

Indore's average yields (930 kg/ha) are a little higher than that of India (834 kg/ha) but fall too short of the USA average of 1540 kg/ha and 1611 kg/ha of Canada. The fluctuations around yield are 23% in Indore (Fig. 3.33)—it is only 7

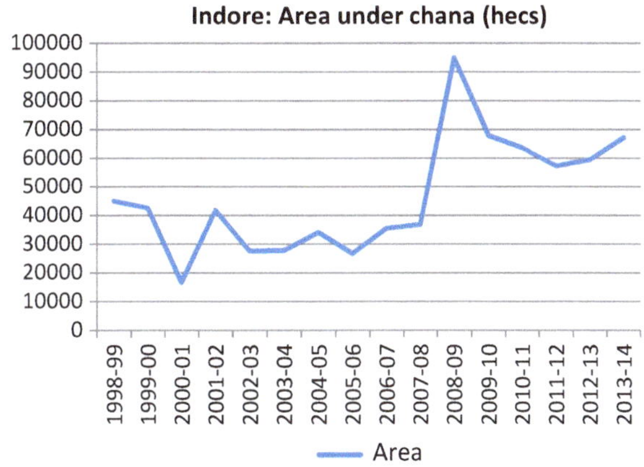

Fig. 3.32 Area under chana in Indore. *Source* Ministry of Agriculture, Government of India (indiastat.com)

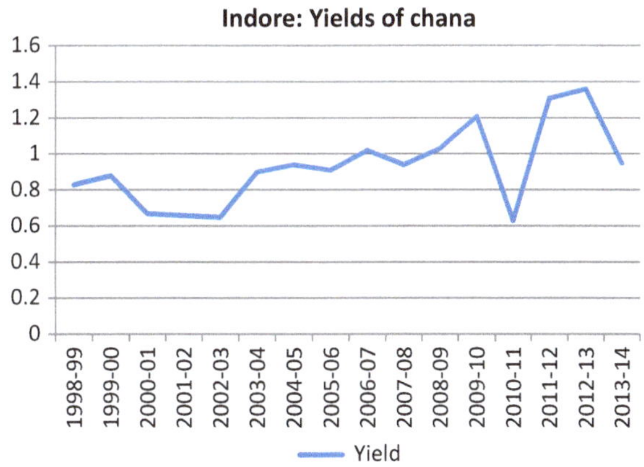

Fig. 3.33 Yields of chana in Indore. *Source* Ministry of Agriculture, Government of India (indiastat.com)

and 6%, respectively, for India and the USA. Thus, what Indore gains in terms of somewhat higher yields, it loses because of such uncertainty. Still, the yields are higher than other pulses and ensure good profit to the farmers. The yields also show a slight increasing trend (the R^2 always come out to be too low for these equations to present a statistical result; but a good t statistics for the variable shows a likely relationship), which must be encouraging farmers to stick to this crop.

3.7.7 Conclusion

All the sample regions growing pulses are from semi-arid tropics. The general productivity (except chana in Indore) is far lower than the national average. The yields are far too volatile—they are much higher than the Indian average. Maybe because of such risks, pulses have started falling from favor in Valsad and East Godavari. The loss in production is too high to be made up by the increased prices.

Interestingly, Jodhpur, in spite of experiencing wild fluctuations in yields, has been putting more area under moong (although our field survey reports to the contrary). Similarly, Indore is also growing more chana than before.

Pulses in India need to be supported for stabler production, mainly in the regions that have comparative advantage in the crop. Also, farmers' issues with animal attacks—pulses seem to be most susceptible to such attacks—should be addressed urgently to increase support to the crop.

3.8 Cotton

Over the years, cotton has seen tremendous rise in production. India used to import cotton in large quantities (8–9 lakh bales per year) in 1970s. Now we are self-sufficient in cotton. After the introduction of BT cotton, the productivity in cotton has also increased notably.

Cotton and some other cash crops are grown on the same land in two seasons—cotton in kharif and the other regional cash crop in rabi. Region-wise analysis for cotton follows.

Region	Yield (kg/ha)	Fluctuations (in yields: mean/STDEV) (%)
Ahmedabad	167	28
Sabarkantha	260	42
Kheda	547.8	24
Junagadh	679.67	39
India	353.27	33
USA	839.93	12

3.8.1 Ahmedabad

The dominating trend in area under cotton is upwards (see Fig. 3.34). The Ahmedabad farmers also confirmed that they did not substitute cotton with any other crop. The yields do not fluctuate widely as shown in Fig. 3.35 (the fluctuations around the mean is 11%[1]). The cotton yields in Ahmedabad are much lesser than the national yields; this is mainly due to the fact that Ahmedabad farmers do not use BT seeds. The fluctuation around the mean is lesser than the national average (25.5%) though. Ahmedabad can benefit by adopting BT cotton. Although the yields seem to become more volatile with BT technology, the loss from these fluctuations is lesser compared to the increases in yields.

[1]There was an outlier in the data for the year 2010–11 (the yields were shown to be almost double than the average) that has been removed.

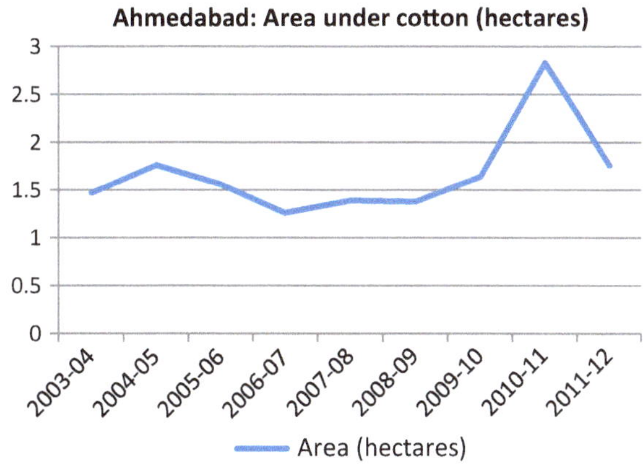

Fig. 3.34 Area under cotton in Ahmedabad. *Source* http://apy.dacnet.nic.in/crop_fryr_toyr.aspx

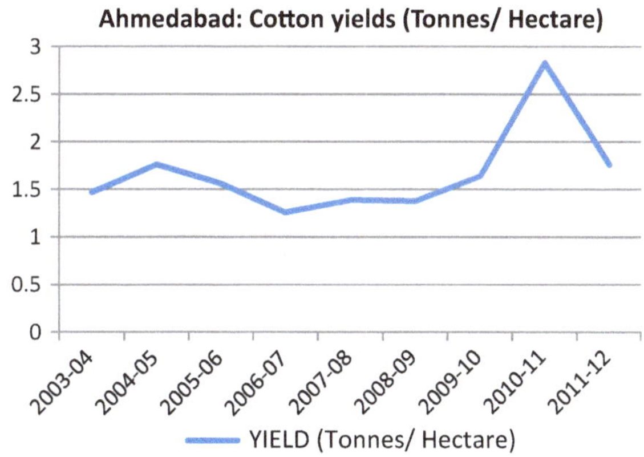

Fig. 3.35 Cotton yields in Ahmedabad. *Source* http://apy.dacnet.nic.in/crop_fryr_toyr.aspx

3.8.2 Sabarkantha

Since 2002, the area under cotton has been only increasing in Sabarkantha (Fig. 3.36). Farmers have been putting more and more area under cotton. However, 26 farmers from Prantij Tehsil (Sabarkantha District) informed us that they rotate the crops. Suppose this year, they grow cotton, then next year, they grow ground nut. Some farmers rotate it within the field: if cotton was grown on plot A and maize on plot B then next year, cotton will be grown on plot B and ground nut on plot A. Also, 20 farmers from south Sabarkantha and 9 farmers from north east Sabarkantha told that depending on the price of cotton and weather conditions, they decide how much cotton they should grow. If weather is bad they avoid growing cotton. 8 out of 29 (27.58%) told they only look at weather, other 7 (24.13%) told they look at price only and remaining 14 (48.27%) told they look at both price and weather conditions.

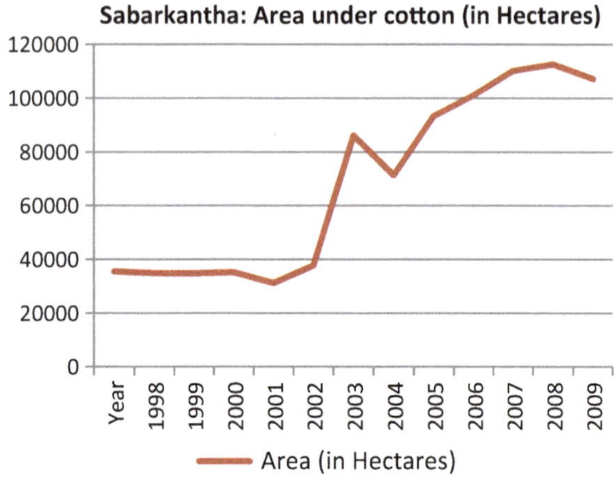

Fig. 3.36 Area under cotton in Sabarkantha. *Source* https://data.gov.in/catalog/district-wise-season-wise-crop-production-statistics

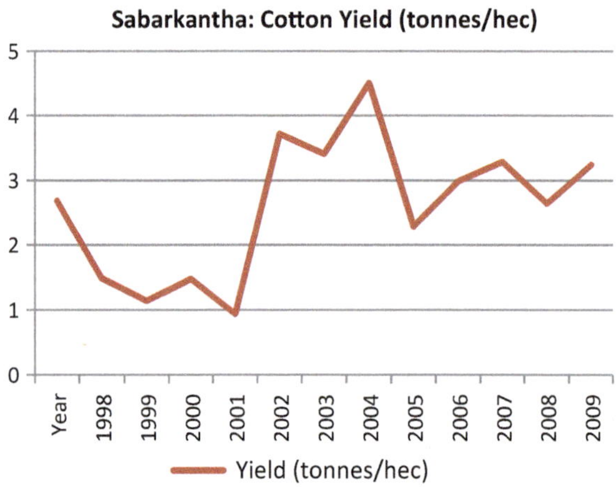

Fig. 3.37 Yields of cotton in Sabarkantha. *Source* https://data.gov.in/catalog/district-wise-season-wise-crop-production-statistics

The average yields (300 kg/ha) are comparable to the national average of 353.57 kg/ha. The fluctuations in yields of 33% around the mean (Fig. 3.37) are also the same as the national average.

3.8.3 Kheda

Since 2005–2006, there are wide fluctuations in area under cotton in kheda (Fig. 3.38). We could not find much explanation from the ground regarding this. 17 farmers from Kheda said that they do not substitute cotton with any other crop. They have been traditionally growing cotton only.

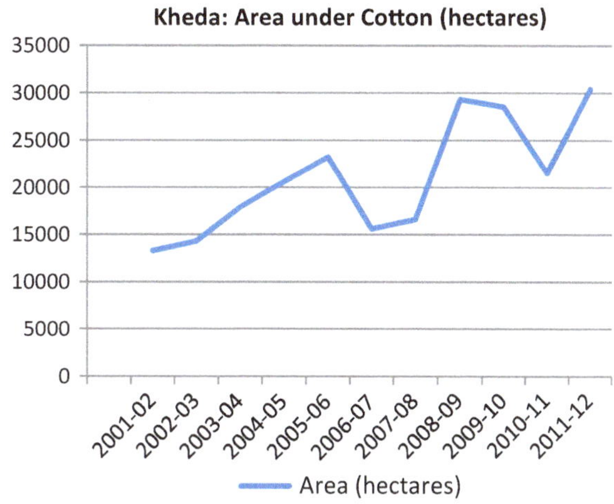

Fig. 3.38 Area under cotton in Kheda. *Source* http://apy.dacnet.nic.in/crop_fryr_toyr.aspx

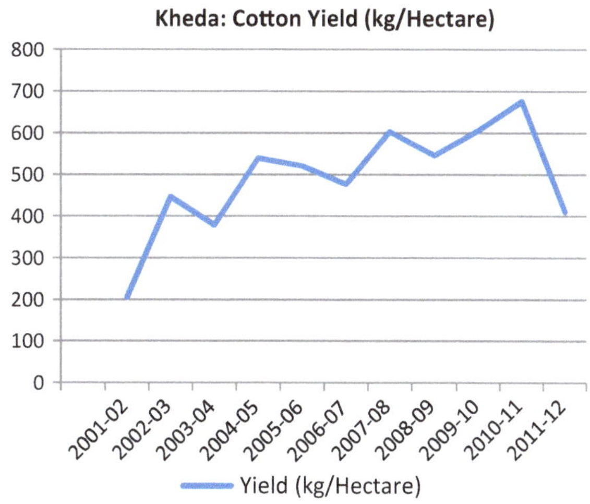

Fig. 3.39 Cotton yields in Kheda. *Source* http://apy.dacnet.nic.in/crop_fryr_toyr.aspx

The average yields of cotton in Kheda (Fig. 3.39) are high: 547.78 kg/ha. This is higher than Sabarkantha and Ahmedabad. It is higher than the national average of 353.57 kg/ha and comparable to the leading cotton states, Andhra Pradesh and Tamil Nadu. The yields have been increasing over the years, as shown in the figure. The volatility is lower at 24% around the mean compared to the national average of 33%. Kheda is known to be agriculturally developed district—the data seems to corroborate this. The district gets better yields than others in almost all crops that it chooses to grow.

However, the productivity is lesser than USA (839.93 kg/ha) and the volatility of yields is also double (24% in Kheda vs. 12% in the USA)

3.8.4 Junagadh

From Fig. 3.40, it is clear that there is an increasing trend in area under cotton in Junagadh—more and more land is brought under cotton. 29 farmers from Junagadh district reported that they have not changed the area under cultivation for cotton for years.

The average yields of cotton in Junagadh (679.67 kg/ha) are more than double of the national average of 334.82 kg/ha and they are somewhat higher than the major cotton grower: Andhra Pradesh and Tamil Nadu. Thus, the productivity is very high in Junagadh. The yields often equal the yields of the advanced nations.

The fluctuation around the mean is 33.4% for India and 39% for Junagadh. The volatility is a bit higher compared (Fig. 3.41) to the national average but given the fact that the yields are far higher, the difference is more than made up. But cotton is a riskier crop compared to the cereals.

The international yields of nations like the USA are higher at 839.93 kg/ha. The fluctuation around the mean is also far lower at 12% as compared to almost 40% for Junagadh. Thus, it seems that the Gujarat farmers might be better in growing cotton

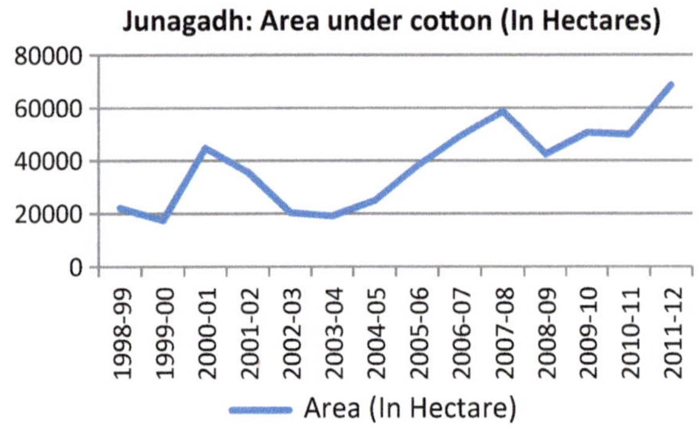

Fig. 3.40 Area under cotton in Junagadh. *Source* http://apy.dacnet.nic.in/crop_fryr_toyr.aspx

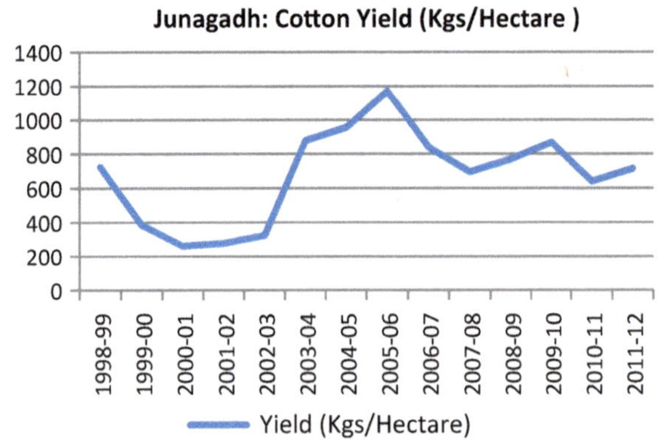

Fig. 3.41 Yields of cotton in Junagadh. *Source* http://apy.dacnet.nic.in/crop_fryr_toyr.aspx

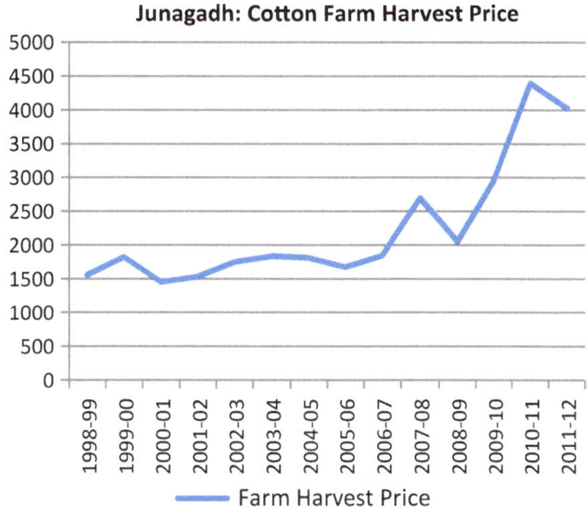

Fig. 3.42 Farm harvest price for cotton in Junagadh. *Source* http://eands.dacnet.nic.in

and understanding the technology better but they compare poorly with the farmers of the world.

There is a strong upward movement in prices in cotton since 2006–2007 till 2011–2012 (Fig. 3.42). However, the price last year (2015–2016) crashed in the world market. Thus, both yield and price risks are higher for cotton. The available data show the risk factor to be high at 41.6% around the mean for prices.

Just like the cereals, the problem is the same with cotton: the productivity is very low compared to the international standards and the volatility is very high. The farmers lose out mainly on production front. In cotton, unlike cereals, the price risks are also high thus the crop for the farmers is profitable but risky at the same time.

3.9 Tobacco

India is the third largest producer of tobacco in the world (The Hindu 2013) It is not a crop that can get government support, but it is a profit making proposition for the farmers. We have studied Anand and Kheda for tobacco where it is a major crop.

Region	Yield (kg/ha)	Fluctuation around mean (%)
Anand	1880	7
Kheda	1717	12
The USA	2160	6

Table 3.6 Area, production and yield of tobacco in Anand

Year		Area (ha)	Production (ton)	Yield (ton/ha)
2004–2005	Whole year	21,800	44,900	2.06
2005–2006	Whole year	22,800	42,600	1.87
2006–2007	Whole year	22,200	39,400	1.77
2007–2008	Whole year	1300	2390	1.83
2008–2009	Kharif	15,600	27,400	1.76
2009–2010	Rabi	13,900	27,200	1.96
2010–2011	Kharif	14,800	29,600	2
	Rabi	62,500	124,600	1.99
	Total	77,300	154,200	1.99
2011–2012	Kharif	12,500	28,100	2.25
	Rabi	62,100	112,200	1.81
	Total	74,600	140,300	1.88

Source http://apy.dacnet.nic.in/crop_fryr_toyr.aspx

3.9.1 *Anand*

Very few farmers were growing tobacco till 2010 (Table 3.6). Since then it has become an important crop. Area and price show good correlation of 0.7. Thus, high prices of tobacco seem to have attracted the farmers. It is interesting that the area under tobacco cultivation has been declining in the USA for the same period. Maybe the anti-smoking campaign has reduced the demand. But the trends certainly are opposite.

In our survey of farmers from Chikhodra and Rasnol villages, we found that tobacco has been providing a stable income for many years to these farmers and hence they have been growing it since last almost 20 years. But for small farmers in Boriyavi, the area under tobacco has gone up. They cited reasons like the stable price of tobacco and relatively low input costs involved which lower the overall risk for the farmers. They also mentioned that unlike potato, it does not suffer from bumper cycles and price crash. That is why they have shifted to tobacco now.

The average yields are 1880 kg/ha. These are not too less compared to 2160 kg/ha for the USA. Thus, the technology adoption seems to be satisfactory. Fluctuations around the mean are 7% for Anand and 6% for the USA. Thus, the crop seems to be relatively stable for the farmer's world around. That weather risks are low is also established by the fact that rainfall and yield correlation is negligible at −0.31.

3.9.2 *Kheda*

Kheda is known by the name golden leaf since it is the chief producer of tobacco in the state. Tobacco grows throughout the year.

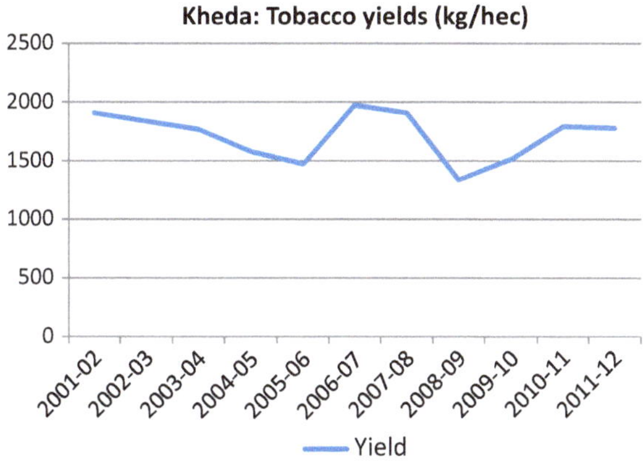

Fig. 3.43 Yields of tobacco in Kheda. *Source* http://apy.dacnet.nic.in/crop_fryr_toyr.aspx

Table 3.7 Area, production and yield in Kheda

Year	Season	Area (ha)	Production (kg)	Yield (kg/ha)
2001–2002	Whole year	64,900	124,200	1910
2002–2003	Whole year	47,400	87,300	1840
2003–2004	Whole year	20,500	36,300	1770
2004–2005	Whole year	30,500	48,200	1580
2005–2006	Whole year	26,400	39,000,000	1475
2006–2007	Whole year	20,700	40,900,000	1975
2007–2008	Whole year	20,200	38,600,000	1910
2008–2009	Kharif	22,500	30,100,000	1337.778
2009–2010	Rabi	35,400	53,700,000	1516.95
2010–2011	Whole year	37,600	67,500,000	1795.21
2011–2012	Whole year	47,700	85,000,000	1781.97

Source http://apy.dacnet.nic.in/crop_fryr_toyr.aspx

The yields fluctuate 12% around the mean (Fig. 3.43). That is slightly higher than Anand. The average yields are 1717 kg/ha which is lower than Anand (1880/ha) and USA (2160 kg/ha).

Between 2003–2004 and 2008–2009, the area under tobacco in Kheda (Table 3.7) remained at a low level. four marginal farmers from Kheda reported to have stopped growing tobacco for many years since the production of tobacco was low and growing the same crop was reducing the fertility of the soil.

But the area is increasing now. Two large farmers from the same region explained how they have addressed that problem of fertility reduction by growing tobacco on different parts of their field. They said that tobacco is a cash crop and earns more profits compared to other crops. The data also shows that prices have gone up considerably since 2008–2009, as shown in Table 3.8.

Table 3.8 Prices of tobacco

Year	Rs./kg
2001–2002	156.1
2002–2003	135.4
2003–2004	172.2
2004–2005	177.7
2005–2006	155.31
2006–2007	170.88
2007–2008	188.93
2008–2009	245.21
2009–2010	238.53
2010–2011	296.42
2011–2012	435.03

Source http://www.eaindustry.nic.in/download_data_0405.asp

The prices of tobacco fluctuate only a little and the major trend is increasing trend.

As a cash crop, tobacco seems to be having little price risk and moderate, if not low, production risk. The Indian productivity as well as yield fluctuations are also not as dismal as some other crops. This seems to be a good crop to grow for farmers; if only it was not so harmful!

3.10 Sugarcane

80% of world sugar is produced from sugarcane. India is the second largest producer of sugarcane in the world (Bee Culture 2016). Gujarat is a smaller player in the sugarcane market in India, compared to UP and Maharashtra. But the southern districts of Gujarat grow sugarcane extensively. We have studied Surat from South Gujarat to understand the uncertainties in sugarcane.

	Surat	Gujarat	India	Brazil
Area fluctuations (%)	8.1	7.4	10	–
Yield risk (%)	7.5	22	5.1	5.5
Ave. yield (ton/ha)	74.11	62.83	67.65	81.46

3.10.1 Surat

The area under sugarcane seems to be quite stable (Table 3.9) with the fluctuations around the mean being just 8.1%. The area under sugarcane for India as a whole

Table 3.9 Area, production and yield of sugarcane in Surat

Year	Area (ha)	Production (ton)	Yield (ton/ha)
1998–1999	113,300	8,326,000	73.49
1999–2000	120,400	8,751,000	72.68
2000–2001	119,000	8,887,000	74.68
2001–2002	113,600	8,521,000	75.01
2002–2003	118,300	8,304,000	70.19
2003–2004	102,700	7,717,000	75.14
2004–2005	116,500	9,071,000	77.86
2005–2006	130,600	11,754,000	90
2006–2007	119,600	9,147,000	76.48
2007–2008	125,900	9,020,000	71.6
2008–2009	112,400	7,974,000	70.9
2009–2010	101,400	7,007,000	69.1
2010–2011	98,900	7,411,000	74.9
2011–2012	105,900	6,942,000	65.55

Source http://apy.dacnet.nic.in/crop_fryr_toyr.aspx

also does not fluctuate much: it is 10% around the mean. Farmers have to look after the sugarcane crop only in the first 4 months in giving fertilizers, etc. After that, they just need to water the crop. Therefore, the area remains stable.

We found that on an average more than two-third land of the sample farmers were covered by sugarcane and other crops are grown in the remaining one-third land on an average. Sugarcane is a popular and important crop for the farmers in Surat.

The National Yield of sugarcane (67.65 ton/ha) is lower than that of Surat (74.11 ton/ha). Surat is doing better than the average yields of Gujarat (62.83 ton/ha), too. Interestingly, the yields are not far lower than the international major player: Brazil (81.46). Thus, Surat has a comparative advantage in growing sugarcane. The reasons could be good quality of soil and good rainfall in this region. Average rain fall measured is 1640 mm in last decade. Also, we feel that government and sugar corporation give good returns in terms of prices to the farmers. This encourages farmers to grow more. Sugarcane is one of the most cultivated crops in this region.

The yield fluctuations around the mean are slightly higher for Surat though (Table 3.9): It is 7.5% for Surat whereas the national fluctuations are 5.1%. Surat's comparative advantage still stays because the difference is yield is more than the difference in volatility.

Volatility at the international level of Brazil in yields (5.5%) is almost the same as the Indian average. Thus Indian farmer seems to have learned the technology well although the yields can be improved further.

Table 3.10 Farm harvest price of sugarcane in Gujarat

Year	Price (Rs./ton)
1998–1999	1167
1999–2000	1181
2000–2001	1182
2001–2002	1239
2002–2003	1191
2003–2004	1240
2004–2005	1346
2005–2006	1623
2006–2007	1551
2007–2008	1486
2008–2009	1351
2009–2010	1942
2010–2011	2260
2011–2012	1900

Source gujstat.com

Farm harvest prices (Table 3.10) also are quite stable with the fluctuations around the mean being 15%. The pricing policy of Gujarat seems to have kept the price risks less. There have been problems with sugarcane pricing in UP and Maharashtra. But Gujarat never came in news about such differences. Thus, sugarcane is a good crop to grow for Surat—it is cash crop so brings in good income, yields do not fluctuate much and the prices also are generally satisfactory.

3.11 Ground Nut

Ground nut accounts for 25% of total oilseed production in the country—it is an important oilseed for India. Gujarat is the largest producer of groundnut in India with more than 50% share in the total groundnut production (Ethical Post 2016). Junagadh belongs to the major groundnut producing region of Saurashtra in Gujarat. We have studied Junagadh to understand the riskiness of the crop.

	Junagadh	Gujarat	India	USA
Yield risk (%)	37	44	21	11
Average yield (ton/ha)	1.58	1.26	1.11	3.34

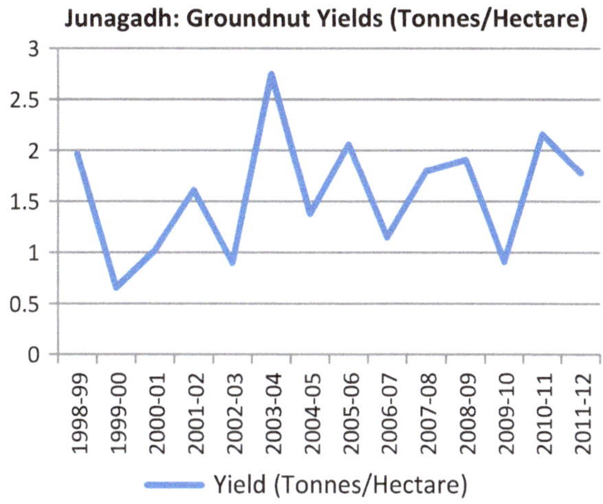

Fig. 3.44 Ground nut yields in Junagadh. *Source* http://apy.dacnet.nic.in/crop_fryr_toyr.aspx

3.11.1 Junagadh

Area under groundnut has remained more or less the same over the years. The fluctuations around the mean (Fig. 3.44) are as low as 4%. Thus, ground nut is a regular crop that the farmers in Junagadh take; they do not seem to change the cropping pattern much for this crop.

Out of 28 farmers surveyed in Junagadh district, for 27 the area under cultivation for groundnut remained the same. The only farmer who said that it has changed explained that because he is into buying and selling of lands and cultivates depending on how much land he has that year. Since Junagadh is famous for its cotton also, we asked the farmers whether anyone wanted to substitute ground nut with cotton. They said that cotton requires more water and more skilled labor. So it was advisable to stick to ground nut. Also, they feel that the Junagadh weather is better suited to grow ground nut.

The yields of ground nuts are quite stagnant—there is no increasing/decreasing trend noted. However, fluctuations around the mean are wild: the productivity can change by 38% in a year!

The average yields of Junagadh (1580 kg/ha) are higher than the average yields of Gujarat (1260 kg/ha) and India (1110 kg/ha). But compared to the USA, whose average yields are 3340 kg/ha, Junagadh is far behind. Fluctuations around the mean for the USA are also almost one-third of Junagadh. Thus, we fare poorly in the international comparison. It would be important to understand from the scientists why this is the case because Junagadh has good resource accessibility and experienced farmers.

Prices are showing a strong upwards movement—with very little downward fluctuations. Thus, prices do not seem to be presenting many problems for the farmers.

3.12 Soybean

Soybean contains very high proportion of protein and has started being used in many parts of the world, including India, for this property. It originally belongs to East Asia. Soybean is used by itself but products made from it, mainly soy oil, soy sauce, tofu, and soy milk are used more than the beans. Madhya Pradesh is a major producer of soybean in India. We have taken Indore to study this crop and its trends.

Region	Yield (kg/ha)	Fluctuation around mean (%)
Indore	1180	18
India	1140	12.5
USA	2830	3.55

3.12.1 *Indore*

Area under soybean has been showing a gradual increasing trend (Fig. 3.45). It is a new crop for Madhya Pradesh but farmers seem to have adopted it well. And more and more farmers seem to be interested in growing it. The ones who had adopted it earlier, are now allotting that land for soybean every year consistently. Therefore, the fluctuations around the mean for acreage under soybean are as small as 3%.

Yields in Indore are 1.18 ton/ha which is comparable to the national average of 1.14 ton/ha. However, like most other crops under study here, soybean productivity also compares poorly with the international average yields of Brazil (2.68 ton/ha) and USA (2.83 ton/ha).

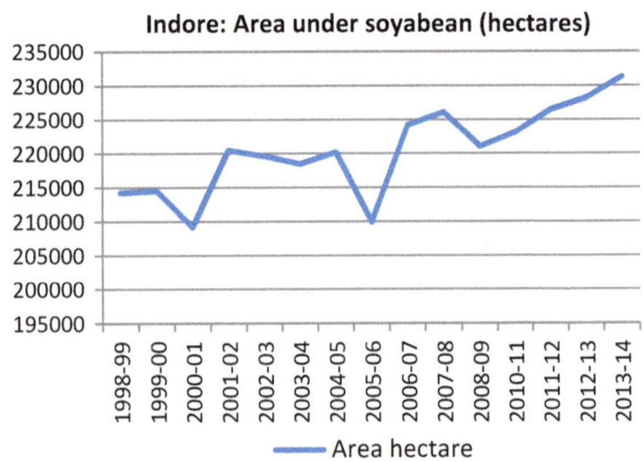

Fig. 3.45 Area under soybean, Indore. *Source* www.agricoop.nic.in

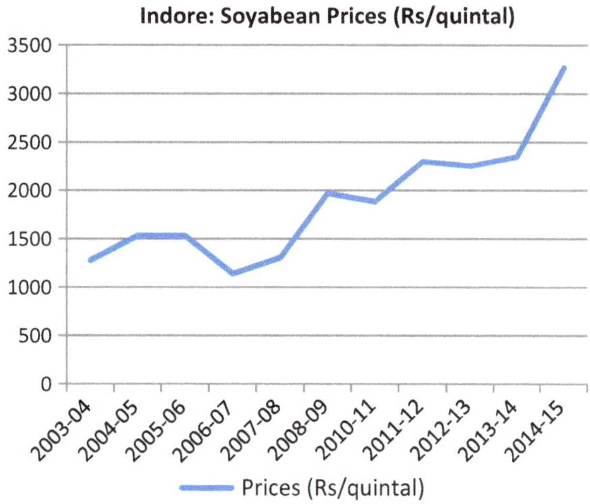

Fig. 3.46 Farm harvest price for soybean, Indore. *Source* http://agmarknet.dac.gov.in/SearchCmmMkt.aspx

The volatility in yields is high at 18% around the mean. For India, the volatility is lower at 12.5%. For the USA, it is just 3.55%. Thus, Indian farmer is more prone to yield losses compared to the American farmer and the Indore farmers are even more prone to yield risks. Given that this crop is very stable in general, it would be useful to try to adopt better methods of growing soybean. Maybe access to reliable irrigation can also improve productivity.

The price risk is not much. The crop is experiencing a generally increasing trend (Fig. 3.46). Soybean is a suitable crop for Indore, it gives average yields and gets reliable prices. However, the yield risks are somewhat higher. We need to work on it.

3.13 Potato

India is third largest nation producing potato. Potato production has been increasing in India in response to demand: between 1960 and 2000, the production increased by almost 850% (http://www.potatopro.com/india/potato-statistics). Gujarat comes among the top five potato producing states in India. We have looked at Kheda to examine the challenges presented by potato.

Region	Yield	Fluctuation around mean (%)
Kheda	21,006	20
India	18,992	11
USA	38,490	5

3.13.1 Kheda

Acreage under potatoes has been declining since 2007–2008 (Fig. 3.47). It is surprising because the yields have been good. However, the potato farmers from Umiya farm (these are all large farmers), the largest producers of potatoes in Kheda, have always cultivated the same crop and do not plan to change it either. They agree that there are wide fluctuations in prices but they say that they have cold storage to take care of that problem. However, farmers during a group discussion in Boriyavi and from Samarkha (Anand district) explained that potato is a high-cost crop. That is why crash in price during bumper crop years hits them hard. They have shifted to tobacco.

Yields are experiencing a gradual declining trend (Fig. 3.48). This needs to be further investigated. The fluctuation around mean is high at 20% (Table 3.11). Such declining yields might have also induced some farmers to give up potato farming.

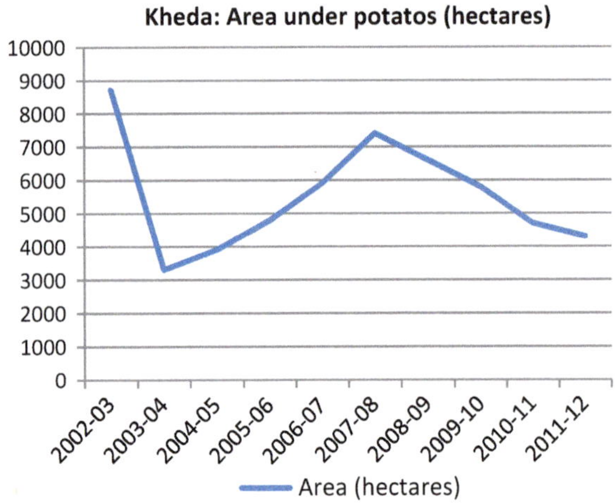

Fig. 3.47 Area under potatoes in Kheda. *Source* http://apy.dacnet.nic.in/crop_fryr_toyr.aspx

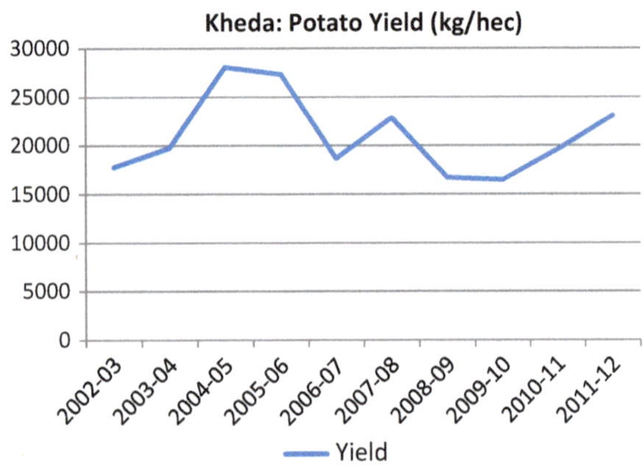

Fig. 3.48 Yields of potatoes in Kheda. *Source* http://apy.dacnet.nic.in/crop_fryr_toyr.aspx

Table 3.11 Area, production and yield of potato in Kheda

	Area	Production	Yield
2002–2003	87	1544	17,747
2003–2004	33	651	19,727
2004–2005	39	1094	28,051
2005–2006	48	1312	27,333
2006–2007	59	1100	18,644
2007–2008	74	1689	22,824
2008–2009	66	1100	16,667
2009–2010	58	954	16,448
2010–2011	47	920	19,574
2011–2012	43	991	23,047
Mean/average	5540	11,355	21,006
Standard deviation	1675	30,616	4171.7
Risk	0.3024266348	0.2696300286	0.198592

Source http://apy.dacnet.nic.in/crop_fryr_toyr.aspx

Table 3.12 Wholesale prices of potatoes, Gujarat

2002–2003	206.5
2003–2004	112.7
2004–2005	159.9
2005–2006	173.43
2006–2007	221.57
2007–2008	223.7
2008–2009	185.82
2009–2010	317.55
2010–11	215.29
2011–12	207.9

Source www.eaindustry.nic.in

Even with such declining trend, Kheda yields are better than the Indian average of 18,992 kg/ha. Fluctuations around the mean are much lower at 11%.

The USA, a major producer of potatoes has much higher average yield of 38,490 kg/ha. The volatility in yields is also far lesser at 5%.

If we set aside the sudden increase in price in 2009–2010, the general trend in prices of potatoes is of gradual increase (Table 3.12). However, this seems to be the average price received over the season. It is well known that potato goes through bumper cycles every third year and the prices completely crash in the market. It is a crop with very high price risk and moderate yield risk. Interestingly, the large farmers told us that since potatoes go through bumper cycles, they look at the average profitability over three years.

3.14 Cashewnut

India is the largest cashew processor in the world. It accounts for 65% of world exports (IBEF.org). Cashew nut was introduced in India by the Portuguese; Goa still produces the tastiest cashews in India. Goa is taken up as a sample district for studying cashew nut.

Region	Yield (kg/ha)	Fluctuation around mean (%)
Goa	372	28
India	740	8.7
Vietnam	3800	33

3.14.1 Goa

Commercial cultivation of cashew is undertaken in eight states—Andhra Pradesh, Goa, Karnataka, Kerala, Maharashtra, Orissa, Tamil Nadu, and West Bengal. The average national yields are 740 kg/ha. Goa's average yields are 372.33 kg/ha (Table 3.13). Thus, the yields are much lesser. But the taste of cashew nuts growing

Table 3.13 Area, production and yield of cashew nut in Goa

Year	Area (ha)	Production (ton)	Yield (kg/ha)
1997–1998	52,204	5220	100
1998–1999	52,875	15,000	284
1999–2000	53,292	17,274	324
2000–2001	53,767	21,335	425
2001–2002	54,060	22,976	425
2002–2003	54,373	23,109	425
2003–2004	54,668	23,233	425
2004–2005	54,858	25,556	466
2005–2006	55,021	27,070	492
2006–2007	55,302	24,380	441
2007–2008	55,612	21,942	395
2008–2009	55,672	13,165	236
2009–2010	55,732	17,556	315
2010–2011	55,732	23,138	415
2011–2012	55,737	23,240	417
Mean	54593.66667	20279.6	372.3333333
STDEV	1141.236777	5715.321573	103.3065249
Risk	0.020904197	0.281826149	0.277457095

Source www.agri.goa.gov.in

in Goa is considered to be far superior to other varieties. Thus, it fetches much higher prices. Exports of Goa cashew are also high. It is felt that cashew yields can increase even further if farmers take more interest in growing it. Cashew requires a lot of expertise; farmers can learn these techniques and earn much more. Kerala and Maharashtra have higher than national average yields; about 1300 kg/ha. India's yields and even Kerala's yields are far lesser than Vietnam's: Vietnam produces 3800 kg/ha.

The fluctuations in yield (28%) for Goa (Table 3.13) are far higher than the national average of 8.7%. The risk in Vietnam is higher at 33%. Major changes that improved yields in Vietnam include, shifts from hilly areas to plains, shift from soil conservation oriented cashew plantation to commercial high density plantation, improved seedlings, proper planting and harvesting schedules and fertilizer and pesticide management (cashew handbook, 2014 - www.cashewinfo.com).

The area under cashew nut has been increasing gradually: it grew slightly from about 52,000 to about 56,000 ha. in last 10 years. 18 farmers from Goa reported that there is no question of changing the area under cultivation for cashew because these are the trees that are present for several years. But not much new land has been brought under cashew either.

Cashew farmers also do not face much price risk since the trend is generally going upwards.

3.15 Coconut

Asia accounts for much of the world's coconut production and India is the third largest producer of coconut in the world (toppost.in), next to Philippines and Indonesia. The southern states are the largest producers of coconut in India but with its long coast line, coconut is an important crop for Goa. The risks faced by the farmers are examined here.

Region	Yield (nuts/ha)	Fluctuation around mean (%)
Goa	4952	1.38
India	10,345	8.7
Indonesia	7752	7

3.15.1 Goa

Area under coconut has been gradually increasing (Table 3.14). Acreage under coconut also does not go down easily because the trees are standing on the land for many years.

Table 3.14 Area, Production and Yield of coconut

Year	Area (ha)	Production (in million nuts)	Yield (nuts/ha)
1997–1998	24,788	120	4841
1998–1999	24,858	121	4868
1999–2000	24,975	121.58	4868
2000–2001	25,025	125.12	4868
2001–2002	25,025	125.12	4868
2002–2003	25,068	122.02	4868
2003–2004	25,110	122.22	4867
2004–2005	25,160	123.52	4909
2005–2006	25,312	125.34	4952
2006–2007	25,468	126.68	4978
2007–2008	25,545	127.57	4994
2008–2009	25,608	128.18	5006
2009–2010	25,686	128.72	5011
2010–2011	25,718	129.88	5011
2011–2012	25,730	129.28	5014
Mean	25,239	124.7821429	4922.071
STDEV	313.637468	3.139917144	65.8979
Risk	0.0124267	0.025163193	0.013388

Source www.agri.goa.gov.in

Average coconut yield is 10,345 nuts/ha in India but the Goan coconut yield is just 4952 nuts/ha (Table 3.14). Coconut gains first fruit in 6–8 years and attains peak production in the age range of 14–20 years. Older trees not only give low yield but are also more susceptible to diseases. The biggest impediment to high yields in Goa is the presence of older trees. It is also believed that with high labor costs in Goa (due to tourism), it is difficult to give enough care to the trees.

India has better yields than Indonesia in coconut (about 7752 nuts/ha: 6.46 ton/ha). India has the highest yields in coconut in the world.

The correlation of coconut yield with water is 0.684. This is because better varieties of coconut require higher quantities of water. Coconut produces nuts round the year. Therefore, adequate supply of water is essential for its unhindered growth. Soil moisture is essential for the absorption of nutrients by roots by proper irrigation equipment. Moisture stress leads to stunted growth, drooping of leaves, immature nut fall and decreased yield. Goan coconut plantations do not have much access to irrigation so here too it suffers.

Indian coconut yield risk is about 0.08929 whereas Goan coconut yield risk is 0.01375. Indonesia has a yield risk of 0.07. There are no downward movements in yields, in that sense the crop is risk free in production.

The price risk for coconut in India was found to be 21.86%, which is quite high. But since the expenditure on coconut is not very high, the changes do not affect the farmers that much.

3.16 Apple

Area under apple has remained more or less the same (Table 3.15). All the 44 farmers interviewed from five villages of Simla District said that they never substitute apples by any other crop. Farmers want to expand their farming land, but there is no vacant arable land available.

The farmers informed us that after a few good seasons, there comes a season when the production decreases. It is a cycle that the apple orchards have and no matter what they do, the production decreases. Table 3.15 demonstrates that it is true. The fluctuations in yields are high—44% around the mean. The yields are 9397.33 kg/ha which are higher than the national average of 7101.7 kg/ha. Simla has comparative advantage in growing apples. The yields in the USA are 4628 kg/ha. Thus, India and Simla have far better average than USA in apple yields.

Fluctuations around the mean though are much higher (44%) for Simla compared to India (24%) and USA (8.7%). However, the lower yields of Simla are equal to the high yields of USA and China. Thus in comparative sense, the farmers should not be worried about the yield risk. Still high yield risk is a matter of concern for the apple farmers. Apple prices fluctuate a lot (38%) so the farmers face high price risk too.

Table 3.15 Area, production and yield of apples in Simla

Year	Area (ha)	Production (MT)	Yield (kg/ha)
1998	33833.41	284483	8408.345479
1999	34421.69	20,536	596.6005736
2000	35008.34	274,000	7826.706436
2001	35905.42	110,857	3087.472588
2002	30,306	229,153	7561.307992
2003	28247.24	294,400	10422.25718
2004	29,029	318,450	10970.06442
2005	30087.69	310,252	10311.59255
2006	30655.18	180,339	5882.823066
2007	31323.24	349,362	11153.4439
2008	31965.68	325,088	10169.90723
2009	33,675	418,900	12439.49517
2010	34721.58	602,684	17357.62025
2011	36036.96	250,372	6947.644862
2012	37264.6	488,525	13109.62683
2013	37552.01	529,888	14110.77596
Standard deviation	2943.453927	148792.5871	4156.08107
Mean	33127.065	311705.5625	9397.23028
Risk	0.08885344737	0.4773497973	0.4422665984

Source Department of Economics and Statistics (http://admis.hp.nic.in/himachal/economics/REPORTS/StatAbstractShimla1314_A1b.pdf)

3.17 Summary and Conclusion

The above analysis shows that out of the 18 crops studied, India has the highest yields in the world in coconut and very low yield risk. Tobacco yields and volatility are quite comparable with other nations. Wheat yields and volatility are comparable to the USA (although yields are much lower than New Zealand) and sugarcane yields and volatility are comparable to an extent with Brazil. The productivity of apples is satisfactorily high in India but the yield risk is much higher too. Still, India is technically competitive in these crops.

Unfortunately, the districts that we took up—most of which were in the semi-arid tropics—had far lesser yields and much more volatile fluctuations in most of the sample crops. Only tobacco and sugarcane growing sample districts were found to be the same level as India and world.

There are crops like cashew nut, chana, jowar, and bajra that have attained relatively better stability in yields than other nations but the yields are far lower. The incomes of farmers would have been much more with higher yields, even if they came with more volatility.

In nine crops out of 18 under study, India and the sample districts fare very poorly—the yields are far lower than the other nations *and* the volatility is far higher. These are potato, soybean, ground nut, cotton, urad, moth, moong, maize, and rice. If appropriate technology is disseminated and adequate resources are made available to the farmers, India should be able to attain far higher levels of agriculture production.

For India, the most volatile yields are experienced in three crops: bajra, cotton, and maize. Generally, it is believed that cereals are low profit, low-risk crops but not all cereals in our study are low risk.

Among the districts, the most risk is faced by the ones that have the least irrigation penetration—Jodhpur and Indore. Simla and Sabarkantha also have substantial lands without irrigation. The yield fluctuations are high for many crops in these districts too. Anand and Kheda, two districts from agriculturally advanced regions, have the lowest fluctuations in yields. Thus, irrigation and proper technology adoption together seem to make a difference in agriculture performance.

Chapter 4
Risk Profile: Findings from the Field

In this chapter, the views and information given by the farmers are used to understand the actual risks that the farmers have to handle. It has been maintained throughout the last chapter that fluctuations in production happen because of natural factors, lesser resource availability or inadequate knowledge of technology. Hence, we start with accessibility to irrigation sources because they help the farmers in getting over the risk of deficient rains—one of the most common occurrences in semi-arid tropics.

Section two lists out the three most important risks identified by the farmers. The risks are described in details for each region so that the farmers' fears are properly understood. Pests and diseases, generally considered as risks, were found to be not high on the list of concerns for the farmers; this has also been explained region-wise.

The government provides risk-proofing measures to protect the farmers from the production and price risks. The third section looks into farmers' attitude toward these measures. This would inform the policy makers about why certain measures are or are not popular.

4.1 Availability of Irrigation

In 5 out of 11 districts, all our sample farmers had irrigation. The remaining six districts differed in the access to irrigation (Table 4.1).

All the field observations reported in this chapter are taken directly from the research reports for different districts written by 11 B.Tech students: Kheda: Valay Vaidya, Anand: Kartikaya Chaturvedi, Surat: Divyesh Chaudhary, Jodhpur: Amit Aseri, Sabarkantha: Rahul Gajjar, Simla: Vivek Kumar Bodh, Indore: Parth Dave, Junagadh: Sandip Ravaliya, Goa: Shashank Singh, Valsad: Saurabh Gunavat, East Godavari: Sai Mithra.

A. Parikh, *Risks in Agriculture*, SpringerBriefs in Economics,
DOI 10.1007/978-981-10-6271-1_4

Table 4.1 District wise availability of irrigation for sample farmers

District	Extent of irrigation availability for sample farmers
Kheda	All sample farmers have it
Anand	All sample farmers have it
Sabarkantha	All sample farmers have it
Junagadh	All sample farmers have irrigation
East Godavari	All sample farmers have irrigation
Surat	31 out of 45 (68%) have irrigation facilities
Valsad	2 out of 4 villages have irrigation; out of the other two, one has partial irrigation
Simla	Apple: rain dependent
	Wheat and maize: (59% have irrigation)
Indore	18 out of 24 had tubewells and yet all are dependent on rain.
Jodhpur	7 out of 68 farmers have irrigation
Goa	No irrigation

4.1.1 Kheda

All farmers had irrigation facilities. Because of the availability of various sources of irrigation the deficient rainfall over the period of time has lost its importance, according to all farmers.

For cotton and tobacco, all the farmers use the water from a borewell. Four farmers buy the water while others have their own borewell. For potato, in Umiya Farm, Sandeepbhai and his partners use the drip irrigation system. When asked in other villages whether drip irrigation is used, one farmer, Ramatubhai shared the farmers' concern about animals walking over the drip irrigation pipelines and damaging them.

Farmers from Radhu believed that in spite of all these facilities, rain is important because the other sources of water that they get is of inferior quality: it is either salty because of the borewell or polluted in the canal because of the industries (there are a lot of industries around the village). But, they opined that it did not make a drastic difference if it does not rain much. It is just that they would *prefer* purer water.

4.1.2 Anand

All villages surveyed in Anand district have been covered by irrigation facilities: borewell, canal, open well, or drip irrigation. A large farmer from Rasnol mentioned that he received a subsidy for digging the borewell and that they are given electricity 8 hours a day to use it. Access to electricity is as important as ownership of tubewell.

4.1.3 Simla

Apples: All apple farmers are completely dependent on the rainfall. Only one farmer uses sprinkler irrigation and that is done only on the area where vegetables are grown.

Maize and Wheat: With the help of government department 3 out of 19 farmers have started using drip irrigation in their fields. 7 farmers use sprinklers in their fields. Seven farmers still use pipes from storage tanks or canals to irrigate their lands. However, the entire owned land is not irrigated. Based on the responses from 16 farmers, we can say that for maize and wheat, on an average 59% of the area is irrigated. The difference in irrigation availability is shown in Table 4.2.

4.1.4 Sabarkantha

The farmers around Prantij tehsil irrigate their land using borewell (groundwater) and farmers in north east area use well as irrigation source—they claimed they get water at 80–100 feet from the surface.

Farmers in Prantij area have Narmada canal, but timing of water release is not reliable, it is not always there when they want. Besides that, one farmer explained that the temperature of canal water is cold and the water they get from borewell is warm. Warm water helps seeds to grow at the maximum rate and roots extend deeper and longer. Warm water is believed to be good for soil too. Extended use of canal water is believed to decrease production and after long use soil gets "cold" hence less production and less fertile soil. Therefore, everyone that we interviewed was using borewell water.[1] They use canal water only when the borewell supply falters.

Electricity is very reliable in this area, 8 hours a day. They have 24 hour electricity at home under Jyotigram Yojna but borewells use three phase high power line. This line is activated twice a day, four hours in the morning and four hours in the evening.

4.1.5 Indore

As there is no river flowing through Indore, the major problem faced by farmers was that of water scarcity. Soybean is a rainfed crop and is dependent on monsoon. Irrigation is mainly done through tube wells but only large farmers can afford to own a tubewell as it costs around 7–10 lakhs. Mr. Sunil Dingu of Rau village, told that only 20% of the water requirements are fulfilled by tubewell and thus they are mainly dependent on rains. The tubewells also run dry often.

[1] We do not know whether there is scientific evidence to support these beliefs.

Table 4.2 Extent of Irrigation on sample farmer's lands in Simla

Sr. No	Total area (ha)	Irrigated land (ha)	Irrigated land/total area
1	2.24	0.32	0.1428
2	2.56	0.16	0.0625
3	3.2	0.48	0.15
4	1.12	0.8	0.7143
5	2.88	1.92	0.667
6	0.96	0.64	0.667
7	1.28	1.28	1
8	5.6	2.72	0.4857
9	1.6	1.12	0.7
10	3.2	1.6	0.5
12	1.28	1.28	1
13	4.8	2.4	0.5
14	4.8	4	0.8333
15	4	4	1
16	2	1	0.5
Average			0.5948

Very few small and medium level farmers can afford tubewells. They have to be dependent on rains. Survey conducted in every sample village showed that water problems were severe and needed urgent attention.

4.1.6 Surat

23 out of the 45 interviewed farmers (51.11%) have irrigation facilities. They get both canal water and borewell water. They report that both sources are reliable. Eight small farmers (17.77%) get surface irrigation only.

4.1.7 Valsad

Out of the four villages, three villages have irrigation with both ground water and canal water.

In Umarsadi they do have canal but it has been dry always. It has been there for 40 years but water was there in it only in two years out of 40. Money is spent for cleaning canal but there is no water in it. So they use borewell. Umarsadi has the system where high power electricity is supplied for 8 hours during day time in one week and in the following week, it is supplied in the night. It is inconvenient for the farmers but at least they do not face the risks of less water.

In Kanjan they do have canal by Kakrapar Yojana and there is regular supply of water. They also use borewells. In Samarpada also, they use well water and also have a canal water from Daman Ganga River. The canal water is released every 15 days. Thus, surface water irrigation is found to be of less use than the ground water irrigation in two out of three villages.

In Khaprada, for farming they only depend on rainfall as the village is located in hilly area. During the group discussion, villagers said just 10% of farmers must be having irrigation. These are rich and influential people like sapanch of village (who were not present for the group discussion).

4.1.8 Junagadh

All groundnut farmers from Ambecha have irrigation. Meghal river, a seasonal river, recharges their wells and 26 out of 28 farmers have open dug wells for irrigation. The remaining two buy water from neighbors. 3 farmers own borewells but use open wells as far as possible. Electricity is available 12 hours a day. Similarly, Madhavanti river charges the wells of the cotton farmers in Kenedipur village: 22 out of 29 farmers have their own wells, five depend on the river water (hence no crop in summer) and while two farmers have access to both river and well water. Electricity is available for 12 hours a day in this village too.

4.1.9 Jodhpur

There is no large-scale irrigation project in all the surveyed villages. The farmers have proposed to build check dams to store water but the proposal is still pending.

Just 7 farmers out of the 68 interviewed have facilities for drip irrigation. All these are large farmers. Even they complain that ground water level is going down day by day. High rates of evaporation also reduce the supply. Thus, irrigation is done with much difficulty. In some villages, underground water cannot be used as it is salty. It will kill the crops.

4.1.10 Goa

Goa relies heavily on four months of consistent rainfall. Since rainfall is fairly reliable, we were told that there was little reliance on any means of irrigation. We find this information to be contradictory because for paddy, we were told that various sources of irrigation are used. But the discussions could not give proper information.

4.1.11 East Godavari

All the farmers interviewed had irrigation facilities. The region has a good canal system from Godavari river. Surveys conducted showed that water is in abundance, but the situation has slightly worsened in the villages of Pithapuram mandal due to ongoing water sharing conflicts between the states. This has led to farmers moving away from rice in Rabi season.

For pulses Urad and Moong, there is not much requirement for water. The water that is left over at the time of harvesting of rice is sufficient for pulses to grow.

4.1.12 Conclusion

Total 291 out of 514 farmers (56.6%) surveyed had irrigation. All the farmers of four out six districts of Gujarat reported to have irrigation. In Surat and Valsad also, 50% or more sample farmers had irrigation. Thus, Gujarat farmers seem to have invested heavily in irrigation. Water markets also exist, so if a farmer does not have a tubewell, s/he can buy water from others. Unfortunately, this investment has not helped in getting better yields or more stable crops, as the secondary data analysis has shown.

Out of the other five, East Godavari is the only district from which all the sample farmers reported to have irrigation facilities. Jodhpur, Goa, and Indore have hardly any irrigation reported and Simla has some. In spite of this, Goa has good production record for rice and Simla for apples and Indore for soybean. Jodhpur fails in all respects. Thus, choice of crop and appropriate technology seem to be very important for good production—just as irrigation. Risk reduction is not only related to irrigation. It is an important lesson to learn.

4.2 Risks that the Farmers Face

4.2.1 Natural Factors

This was identified as the most important risk that farmers face. It could be untimely or excessive rainfall, hailstorms, strong winds or any such factor. Farmers on an average lose at least 15% revenue every year due to the weather related factors, if not more or all.

4.2.1.1 Kheda

28 farmers from Bavralaat and Khumarvaad, Kheda district, in a group discussion, informed us that if there is an unseasonal rain, it affects the crops, such as cotton

and tobacco. 17 Cotton farmers in Bavralaat informed that extreme conditions such as hailstorm or excessive rain severely affected the crops and led to less production and sometimes, no production at all. Rupaji, a large farmer of cotton said that too much heat also can burn the cotton crop. This year, because of unseasonal rain in March, there has been a loss of production in tobacco in Khumarvaad. Bajra can also be destroyed by unseasonal rains, i.e., if it rains within 3 days of sowing, the entire crop is destroyed. This has been a major worry for the bajra farmers.

Tobacco, potato and banana farmers in Kheda opined that there is no effect of temperature on their crops.

4.2.1.2 Anand

Bharatbhai, a large farmer from Rasnol in Anand, said that if it becomes extremely cold or when there is a hail storm the entire produce of tobacco is spoilt. This information was missed out by the Kheda tobacco farmers. However, he explained that the region does not regularly experience temperature variations to that degree, so the risk due to temperature though can be potentially catastrophic is not very significant. That must be the reason why the Kheda farmers did not talk about it.

4.2.1.3 Sabarkantha

18 out of 26 farmers in Sabarkantha reported that unseasonal rains are a problem. Wheat gets black spots and then it starts getting white insects in it. No one would buy such wheat from them. Farmers from both Prantij and Vadali tehsil who grow cotton confirmed that weather is a major problem in the case of cotton: Unexpected rain ruins the crop.

For maize, if they sell the fresh maize, they get lesser price. If they decide to sell dry maize, there is a risk of unexpected rainfall ruining all the maize lying on the field. The maize plant also gets severely affected by strong winds: the plant is heavy from upper part so when strong winds blow, the plant falls down and gets destroyed.

4.2.1.4 Surat

24 out of 45 sugarcane farmers (53.33%) in Surat reported that unseasonal rainfall is the most important threat to the production. 6 out of 45 (13.33%) farmers reported that because of unseasonal rainfall in 2013 and 2014, there was the total destruction of the kharif rice crop. Three farmers reported that last year their fields were hit by tornado so the production went down by 30–40%.

4.2.1.5 Valsad

In Khaprada, Valsad, Urad gets affected when too much rains come.

4.2.1.6 Simla

The apple farmers said that too much fluctuations in the temperature lead to decrease in production. Tashi Palzom from Sarahan (Simla) said that sudden decrease in temperature before the budding season leads to failure of the buds to mature properly. This factor decreases the production. Increase in humidity was also reported as one of the factors leading to leaf fall.

Hails have been one of the biggest natural threat for apple farming (28% said so). All the 44 Simla farmers said that hails are the biggest natural factor that affects production. Hails have the strength to reduce production by over 50%. All the 44 farmers were affected by the hails in 2009 and 2011. According to the Horticulture Department of Simla, the production was less by 70% in 2009–2010 compared to the previous year due to hailstorm. It was 50% in 2011–2012 due to both heavy rains and hails. Use of nets to protect the trees is a protective measure that most farmers have, there are also anti-hail guns but they are not very much reliable as hails can hit anytime of the day. One farmer who had managed to cover all the trees with nets suffered 0% loss due to hails. Two other farmers who had used nets, but were not able to cover all the trees reported that they suffered lesser losses from the hails compared to other farms.

Maize and wheat in Simla also suffered from these disasters and the loss was about 60% for one farmer; 40% for another farmer. Heavy unseasonal rainfall is another major risk for these crops.

4.2.1.7 Indore

Surveys in Indore indicated that less rainfall was the most important risk for them. All 15 farmers of Sitapad (Indore) reported hailstorm also to be a major threat to their crops. Drying up of gram (fafoon) was another problem that they reported.

4.2.1.8 Jodhpur

In Jodhpur, less rainfall kills the crop since they have no irrigation sources. If heavy rains come before time, the fields get waterlogged. If rains come during the harvest time, the standing crops get destroyed. But mainly less rains and untimely rains were recognized as major problems.

4.2.1.9 Junagadh

In Junagadh, 25 out of 28 farmers reported natural factors to be responsible for reduction in production. Time and extent of rainfall were indicated to be a crucial factor. Too much rains would rot the seeds, too little rainfall would stunt the growth and rain at harvest time would affect the crop as well as the fodder part of the plant.

All 28 wheat growing farmers emphasized the importance of enough rains for their crop (ground nut grows in kharif and wheat in rabi). Lack of water can lead to decrease in production. 29 cotton farmers talked about untimely rainfall and strong winds as major climate factors affecting their cotton crop.

4.2.1.10 Goa

In Goa, 50% of the farmers have mentioned unfavorable weather conditions for failure of the cashew and coconut crop. Sudden changes in temperature may lead to early ripening of cashew fruits leading to low yield and immature fruit dropping. Unseasonal rainfall or high-speed winds also contribute toward the farmer's woes as the cashew flowers may drop.

4.2.1.11 East Godavari

The farmers of East Godavari said that because of irrigation, rainfall was not a major issue for them but the cost of irrigation was. They do not know for how long they will be able to sustain the expenditure. Then the rainfall would become a major factor affecting production.

4.2.1.12 Conclusion

In the villages which did not have irrigation, less rainfall was a sure risk. Every village surveyed had a problem with excessive or untimely rainfall. This explains the poor correlation or often negative correlation that we got of rainfall with yields.

In the villages that didnot have irrigation, less rainfall was a serious risk. Additionally, strong winds and hailstorm seem to be two important but not uncommon risks from nature. 73% of the surveyed farmers said that these and extreme temperatures can affect their crops adversely. The remaining farmers said that these factors did not affect them that regularly or severely.

In short, a majority of the farmers surveyed have identified natural factors as the most important threats to their production.

The farmers from Valsad talked at length about the "risks" of nearby urbanization—their water was getting polluted and hence productivity was declining. Similarly, the farmers of East Godavari were worried about the "risks" of increasing costs of irrigation. At policy level, these factors also need attention.

4.2.2 Animals

4.2.2.1 Kheda

Be it in *a* group or individual interview, *all* the sample farmers in Kheda mentioned that animals are dangerous for their crops. Animals like pigs, nilgai, and monkeys walk on the crops and also eat it. Large farmers of Umiya Farm and Rupaji from Bavralaat, Kheda, feel that majority of the damage happens because of animals and mentioned that government has not been successful in dealing with the animals.

4.2.2.2 Anand

The menace of animals is a constant and serious concern of all farmers in Anand too. Monkeys, nilgai, and pigs are some of the animals that destroy the crops. The problem is very frequent hence some of the farmers, according to Bharatbhai from Rasnol, have started fencing their lands to protect it from the animals, but owing to the high cost of fencing the farmers carry out the activity in a phased manner. Farmers informed us that the cost can go up to Rs. 35,000 per bigha.

4.2.2.3 Sabarkantha

20 out of 26 farmers in Sabarkantha reported that animals ruin wheat. One farmer in a group discussion reported that his maize area has gone down because of animal risk. Animal problem is higher in villages close to the city so people cultivating around that area have stopped growing maize. In northeast region, they have lesser animal problems. They also use crackers to scare animals at night time.

4.2.2.4 Valsad

In Umarsadi, Valsad, the farmers reported large losses due to pigs.

4.2.2.5 Surat

9 sugarcane farmers from Surat (20%) whose lands are near the jungle have cited the fear of tiger, leopard, wild hog, deer, etc. It was explained to us that sometimes use of pesticides kill snakes too, leading to increase in the population of rats. 11.11% farmers from our sample spoke of the rat problem. The jowar farmers informed us that the birds eat up jowar so once the crop is nearing harvest, they have to be on the field for the whole day to look after the crop; they cannot do anything else.

4.2.2.6 Junagadh

In Junagadh, 4 out of 28 farmers reported that wild animals are affecting ground nut crop. These four also told us that even the wheat crop gets affected.

4.2.2.7 Simla

Monkeys and Parrots are the major animal threats for the apple farmers as the monkeys pluck the flowers in the budding stage or once the apple has grown. Parrots destroy the apples once the apples have grown. 50% of the farmers reported this problem—35% by parrots and 15% by monkeys. One farmer said that the loss due to monkeys can be 40% of the crop.

4.2.2.8 Jodhpur

In Jodhpur, the farmers who grow moong and moth have realized that pigs and neelgai love these crops and they totally eat it up. 37 farmers out of 68 surveyed have given up cultivating the pulses because of the animal menace. Pulses attract pests much faster than cereals so the storage losses are also high.

4.2.2.9 Goa

In Goa, 2 out of 18 farmers identify animal attacks for the destruction of crops. Three out of 19 paddy farmers also complain about animals. Animals such as peacocks, nilgai, and wild boars often enter the fields and damage the crop. The crop damage by animals is considered as quite high. The cashew farmers specifically mention peacocks, other birds, and monkeys as the cause of destruction.

4.2.2.10 East Godavari

Surprisingly when asked about the major risk that they face, all the farmers of East Godavari answered, “animals” instead of rainfall or pests. All the 14 farmers interviewed said that they could tackle the risk of pests and rainfall through pesticides and irrigation, respectively. However, when it comes to animals like monkeys and pigs, they had no solution. In spite of building fences around their fields, the animals would somehow jump over the fences or creep below it and damage the crops.

4.2.2.11 Conclusion

In seven out of ten districts studied, farmers reported animals as a major menace. In other three also, it was reported as a problem although not a serious one. On the whole, 57% farmers reported animals to be a major problem.

Destruction by animals cannot be an unsolvable problem; fencing, some preventive sounds, lights, etc. can be used to keep away the animals from attacking the crops. Unfortunately, hardly any attention has been paid to this major problem that the farmers face. No effective solutions are designed. This is an area that needs immediate attention.

4.2.3 *Pest/Diseases*

4.2.3.1 Kheda

All the farmers from Kheda told that they do not face any problem with the pests since they have been farming and using pesticides for a very long time. However, the Deputy Sarpanch of Khumarvaad, Kheda district, Melabhai Dabhi said that the villagers had not been trained about various fertilizers and the information they had was very limited. He further said that for the marginal farmers who grew tobacco, it was impossible to understand what each letter in NPK stood for and such information about the fertilizers would certainly be helpful, if given.

All 12 tobacco farmers from Khumarvaad, Kheda, mentioned a disease called "Aakumba", a Gujarati word, that affects their tobacco crop (a disease that causes the tobacco leaves to wilt and crumble) because of which they see less production. A large farmer from Rasnol (Anand) and the marginal farmers from Samarkha (Anand) also said that their tobacco plants are hit with "Akumba". The disease generally strikes in December and as yet, the farmers have no way to counter it. However, the loss is not much.

4.2.3.2 Anand

Similarly, Manubhai Dabhibhai and Rupaji, Anand district, in a group discussion with cotton farmers, talked about a disease called "Sukharo" that affects Cotton in such a way that the crop dries up. We could not ascertain the reason for such diseases occurring. Fortunately, the disease has not affected the production much. In general, they said that the risk from pests is low.

4.2.3.3 Simla

19% of the apple farmers from Simla report diseases like:

(a) Mite: where the insect eats the leaf and increases leaf fall
(b) Scale: Insect affects the whole plant including the fruits
(c) Hulia Fit: where the insect named "Borer" eats up the roots and makes the tree weak.

4.2.3.4 Sabarkantha

17 out of 29 farmers in Sabarkantha district (58.62% from Prantij and Vadali tehsil) mentioned that they get pests in cotton crop, that is why cotton is very risky crop for them. One farmer from Chhadarda (Prantij tehsil) said that "Cotton crop likely to fail 80% this year because of pest."

4.2.3.5 Surat

13 out of 45 rice farmers from Surat said that there is no high risk of the crop getting affected by pests. It is not a worry for them. All the jowar farmers reported that pests do not present much risk.

4.2.3.6 Indore

The soybean farmers of Indore reported that damage can be caused by guddle beetle insect which attaches on soybean 15–20 days after sowing. But the crop damage does not seem to be much. Furthermore, there appears to be high level of awareness among farmers on consequences of the indiscriminate and skewed use of chemical fertilizers.

4.2.3.7 Junagadh

Only 5 out of 28 groundnut farmers in Junagadh identified pests as a factor that reduces productivity. On the contrary, all 29 cotton farmers reported that "raatad" (most probably it is the pink ballworm) was major risk to their cotton crop.

4.2.3.8 Goa

7 out of 18 (39%) farmers in Goa mention pests as a risk for cashew and coconut crop. Commonly infected parts of cashewnut include stems, roots (Stem and Root

Borer), fruit (Fruit and Nut Borer), and leaves (Leaf miner). These problems are visible early on when combative measures can be taken. 6 out of 19 (32%) paddy farmers talk of pest problems. Farmers have claimed losses in paddy yields to be 10–15% due to leaf blast, sheath rot, stem rot and the yellow mottle virus. The most common disease in coconut is the Bud rot disease (57% farmers reported this). Other common diseases include leaf rot, root wilt, and stem bleeding. These diseases often spread and then destroy the entire plantation.

4.2.3.9 Jodhpur

In Jodhpur, 58 out of 68 farmers talked about the pest problem during storage for moong and moth. Interestingly, their biggest concerns while growing the crop remained drought/untimely rains and animals. Pests were not considered that important.

4.2.3.10 East Godavari

Just like for rainfall, the farmers of East Godavari said that pesticides took care of the pest problems but the cost of pesticides is becoming too high. So they do not know for how long they will be able to sustain the expenditure and ward off the risk.

4.2.3.11 Conclusion

Risks from pests are faced by all the sample farmers but only 28% of the total report it as a major concern. Most farmers say that pesticides are able to more or less address the problem.

4.2.4 Price Risks

4.2.4.1 Bumper Crop Cycle for Potato and Its Effects

Potato has a bumper crop cycle because of which once in a few years, there would be excessive production. Prices would go down. Since the input costs are high, the losses can be considerable. Maybe this dissuades the smaller farmers from growing potatoes. However, large farmers store the produce in cold storage and wait for the desired price. Bumper crop is not so much of a problem for them.

Bharatbhai from Rasnol gave us an interesting insight: he said that the large farmers in Gujarat have built storage facilities—the largest in the area being his own, one with six godowns. The facility is fully covered from all sides, is made with concrete and is rainproof. The cost of construction of such a unit is very high but it provides the farmers an opportunity to store their produce without risk of any loss and then sell the crop only when they get acceptable prices.

As discussed in the earlier section on acreage, most farmers were growing cotton for long and they did not change to other crops easily in spite of the volatility in prices. Even if price decreases somewhat, it might not be resulting in losses. While asked about this on the field, the farmers from Kheda informed us that they did not sell the cotton in the market and they sold it to the local vendors. Hence, the prices did not change that much for them. In other words, the price fluctuations were more of a risk for the wholesaler than the farmers. The farmers were always given the minimum possible price.

For most crops examined in this study, the prices have been going up every year. Thus, price risk did not seem to be very high for the farmers for the crops studied. Some crops like wheat and maize in Simla, are grown mainly for home consumption. The fluctuations in prices do not affect the farmers.

4.3 Seed Quality

Seed quality did not emerge as a significant risk at all. None of the farmers that we talked to complained about the seed quality.

In Kheda, we were told that the quality of seeds depends on the brand which they buy. In Anand, either farmers make their own seeds or buy them from the well-known brands. Thus, the seed quality is assured.

The sugarcane farmers in Surat say that the sugarcane factory provides them with better and reliable saplings at a subsidized rate (one-fourth the cost). Disease resistant power of these seeds is also high. The seed quality is not much of a concern for the jowar farmers. They buy it from a government agency, Agro and the seed quality is guaranteed.

In Jodhpur, the government shop gives good seeds at subsidized price but we found that only the ones with political influence or having higher status in society get the subsidized seed from the government shop. However, all farmers were happy with the quality of seeds available to them from private shops.

In Simla, the government provides seeds for wheat and maize, thus ensuring the quality.

45 out of 51 farmers (88.23%) in Sabarkantha purchase seeds from private shops. Other 6 farmers (11.76%) get subsidized seeds from the government. The quality of subsidized seeds is also good. In general, no one gets low-quality seeds.

Similarly, Indore farmers report that they have no complaints regarding the seed quality.

The cashew nut farmers in Goa use the local variety seeds only; hence are not worried about the quality and reliability. The local seeds give lesser yields but better taste and therefore there is a high demand for them in the domestic as well as international markets. They fetch higher price also. Similarly, farmers select the seedling from a high yielding and disease free mother palm from their fellow coconut farmers—they do not have to worry about buying it from outside. 15 out of

19 rice farmers buy the seeds from designated government outlets and are very satisfied with the seed quality.

The farmers of East Godavari report that they never compromise on the quality of seeds. All the farmers said that they buy the best available seeds from the market. They change the brand of seeds after every season. It is believed that this helps in maintaining the land fertility.

Only 5 out of 29 farmers (17.24% from Prantij and Vadali tehsil of Sabarkantha district) in our entire survey talked about production getting affected because of low-quality seeds but they also admitted that it does not happen often. One farmer from Chhadarda (Prantij tehsil) told that seed manufacturers have previous year's unsold seeds that they stamp as new and sell. The quality of cotton seeds decreases over time so such seeds can lead to losses for farmers. But such occurrences are few.

4.4 Ranking of Risks

The most important risk that the farmers across all sample districts face (Table 4.3) is that of weather—excessive or untimely rains, hailstorms and extreme change in temperatures. 73% of the sampled farmers identify this as the main risk.

Strangely the second most important risk that farmers face (Table 4.3) has no protection or policies—destruction by animals. 57% farmers have stated that animals are a major risk for them. Fencing is too expensive and they do not know of any other way to stop the animals from entering the fields. This concern of farmers needs to be urgently addressed by the researchers.

Pest attacks were interestingly found to be a cause for loss by just 28% farmers. Pesticides have been able to stop the spread of pests. Thus, pests pose a problem that the farmers usually have a solution for.

Price risk—risk of sudden fall in prices—was faced by just two out of 18 crops under study. None of the farmers identified this as a risk on their own. Potatoes and cotton are the only crops where price volatility can affect incomes.

4.5 Risk Proofing

As discussed in the introduction, insurance cover can address the problems of price and yield fluctuations. Weather based insurance or crop insurance can be helpful when there is damage due to natural disasters. Price risks are considerably reduced

Table 4.3 Risks faced by farmers

Risks	Percentage of farmers reporting it (%)
Weather	73
Animals	57
Pests	28
Price	Only farmers of cotton and potatoes

with the help of Minimum Support Price. The following paragraphs show how effective/ineffective these two risk mitigating measures are.

4.5.1 *Insurance Cover*

One way to tackle the losses and the unpredictability of the weather is to cover your crop with crop insurance. Investigations were made to check whether the farmers of different village have an insurance cover or not. We found that only 17% of the sampled farmers had crop insurance. The following paragraphs explain why others are not interested.

4.5.1.1 Kheda

From the total number of *28* farmers surveyed from Khumarvaad and Bavralaat (Kheda), not a single had crop insurance. In fact, 3 tobacco farmers had no clue about any of the insurance scheme and they mistook the question for various crop loans. However, two others in the group knew about the new insurance scheme namely "Pradhan Mantri Fasal Beema Yojana" but did not have the crop insurance. The general opinion was, "There is a lot of paper work. Plus, there is no guarantee that we would get the claims." In addition to this, a marginal farmer conveyed that they did not even have the money to run the house and that they could not afford any more expenses in any form. He was referring to the premium that the farmers had to pay in order to get insured. While, a big cotton farmer from Bavralaat, told that even they did not have any crop insurance because he has not seen anyone benefitting from it.

The Umiya farm (Kheda) had 28 large farmers. Their opinion was even more straightforward: "For a compensation of Rs. 1000 per Bigha, we would not take the pain of filling 50–100 papers." One of the farmers said, "There are hardly any losses in the crop. Our main worry is to cover the input prices that are too much. Even if we get ourselves covered by an insurance, we would not get much benefit and would lose the money that we paid as the premium." Similarly, all 11 farmers from Radhu village did not have insurance. The reason behind all the farmers not taking the crop insurance was the fact that in the last 10 years, there had been no loss due to unforeseen circumstances. In fact, banana crop has always been profitable.

4.5.1.2 Anand

In Anand, marginal farmers from Boriyavi said that they did not bother to look at insurance schemes as they did not think it would be of benefit to them and cited never ending paperwork as a deterrent. Two large farmers stated that they did not need the insurance for the crops. He could survive without the insurance; there is no need to pay the premiums. None of the farmers of Samarkha knew of the insurance schemes and they were not interested in finding about "any of these government schemes." In Chikhodra, all the farmers were aware of the crop insurance schemes but said that excessive paperwork and documents needed made them shy away from getting one.

4.5.1.3 Sabarkantha

Farmers in Chhadarda (Prantij tehsil, Sabarkantha): 87.50% of farmers have crop insurance but only 50% of them pay premium regularly. They have a Mandali, the insurance is given based on the loan. Remaining 12.5% do not have any insurance. The insured get compensation but it is a long procedure, sometimes it takes even a year to get the claim.

None of the 11 farmers from Hadiyol (Prantij tehsil) have insurance. They had insurance two years ago but after insurance system went online they do not know how to pay premium so they have stopped paying premiums. Out of 25 farmers in north east area, only 3 farmers (12.00%) had insurance but they do not pay premiums so it is the same as having no insurance.

4.5.1.4 Indore

In Indore (Madhya Pradesh), the government has made crop insurance compulsory, if the farmers want to avail of any government subsidies. Therefore, all 24 farmers surveyed had insurance. However, the farmers reported that they receive hardly any benefits from the insurance. Hence actually they do not care about it. In Jamli village, farmers who did not have insurance told us that they grow very little so for them insurance is a waste of money.

4.5.1.5 Surat

Only 8 out of 45 farmers knew about crop insurance in Surat. 30 farmers felt that crop insurance is unnecessary: sugarcane is a steady crop and they always get good prices from cooperative societies. We were told that natural calamities like heavy rains for a week or tornado do not affect the sugarcane crop much. Sugarcane stalks are made up of several segments known as joints. When heavy winds bend down the plants, the joints that fall on the grounds develop new roots and live on. Thus, the total damage is not more than 15–20% of the production. That is one more reason why sugarcane farmers are not interested in insurance.

4.5.1.6 Valsad

In Umarsadi, Valsad, people have not taken loans from banks. When they need money, they sell some land—it is easier and lucrative. Since they do not take loans, they do not get the attached insurance cover either. They also feel that the insurance would not cover mango and other vegetables so it is not of much use for them. In Khaprad, farmers have taken loans but they do not know that the insurance covers come with it. So they have never used it.

4.5.1.7 Jodhpur

29 farmers out of 68 in Jodhpur district had gotten their crops insured (out of the 29, 4 were large farmers and the remaining 25 were small farmers). Strangely the farmers were very secretive about the insurance; they did not want to reveal anything or even discuss it. This included information on claims filed, claims reimbursed, etc. Everyone just kept on changing the topic or simply said that they do not remember the amount of premium paid. It was difficult to understand what was going on and what the ground truth was. The only thing that they revealed was that the claims took 1–3 months to settle—if you knew people in the bank/insurance company, it would take about a month; otherwise anytime between 2 and 3 months.

4.5.1.8 Junagadh

25 farmers out of 28 farmers in Junagadh have crop insurance on their land. All these 25 farmers got compensation in 2014 when a plant disease had spread and destroyed the whole production. It took 2–3 months to settle the claims.

4.5.1.9 Goa

None of the farmers in Goa had crop insurance, though 8 farmers (44.4%) had heard about it. They did not get insured as they felt the process was complicated and they would have to pay a premium. A farmer remarked that every year's production is more or less the same, and hence he considers crop insurance unnecessary.

4.5.1.10 Simla

None of the apple farmers in Simla have crop insurance, neither do the maize and wheat farmers. The apple farmers say it would be very time consuming to get the insurance and even to go and claim it. The maize and wheat farmers get their premiums cut when they borrow from KCC. However, except one farmer none other knew that it is cut. Even he has never claimed anything yet. The large farmers told the interviewer that they can bear the losses but are not interested in insurance.

4.5.1.11 East Godavari

Insurance is made compulsory by the East Godavari (Andhra) government if farmers want to take benefits of government schemes and subsidies. There is good awareness among people about insurance schemes. The government provides insurance schemes to farmers at a subsidized cost. The process of taking insurance is also very simple with the insurance company reaching out directly to farmers. All the farmers who had more than 3 acres of land took insurance in this region. The farmers with an area less than 1 acre did not take insurance cover as they felt it is a waste of money and that money can be better used elsewhere. It is important to note that most of the farmers are not satisfied with the current insurance scheme provided by the government. The insurance claiming process is a very slow process. Three farmers who received money through insurance said that it took almost 1 year for them to get the money. In the best case, one farmer received the money within 3 months.

4.5.1.12 Conclusion

Out of 11 districts, farmers of only 4 districts said unanimously that they did not have insurance—these were Kheda, Anand, Surat, and Goa. Interestingly, tobacco, banana, and sugarcane that are extensively grown here are considered as stable crops and they do not need any insurance usually. They also talked about excessive paperwork and complete mistrust of government procedures. Many were not even aware of the concept of insurance.

For farmers in Khaprad village of Valsad and for many farmers of Simla who had taken loans from the bank, should be paying for insurance but they were not aware of it. Hence, they had never put up any claims. Insurance is as good as not existing.

All farmers in Indore and East Godavari and almost 90% farmers in Junagadh had insurance. Farmers in Junagadh say that they have benefited from it. In East Godavari also, the claims have been settled but only after much delay. In Indore, hardly anyone has received any benefit from insurance so no one cares about it. They have no choice but to be a part of it but for them, it is as good as non-existent.

About 40–50% of farmers had insurance in Jodhpur and Sabakantha. But the farmers say that they are not regular in paying the premium—the reason seemed to be a lack of interest and lack of conviction that it is useful—so the insurance is not of much use to them. In Jodhpur, the farmers were very secretive so nothing much could be learned.

In short, in 8 out of 11 districts, insurance does not seem to be working well. Unless there is a strong demonstration of its use, it is felt that it would not be very helpful in meeting the production risks of the farmers.

4.5.2 *Minimum Support Price (MSP)*

The government guarantees to buy the farmer's entire produce at minimum support price, if the farmer decides to do so. The prevailing market prices do not matter in this guarantee. If the farmer decides to use this facility, the government has to buy his produce—it cannot say no. The farmer uses this offer whenever prices in the market crash. Selling at minimum support price would at least guarantee reasonable returns to the farmers. It is like an insurance given for price—an assurance that the farmer would never have to receive lesser price than this and his losses would be minimal.

The government assures MSP for 25 crops. However, not many sample farmers reported that they are dependent on MSP or that they find MSP to be supportive of their incomes.

4.5.2.1 Kheda and Anand

The tobacco farmers of Kheda and Anand informed us that there is no MSP for tobacco. A large farmer from Anand felt no need for MSP for tobacco, because he uses his cold storage in case of price crash and sells it later. Other farmers said that they always get stable price for tobacco.

All the 17 large farmers who grow cotton in Bavralaat, Kheda had not heard of having any sort of MSP cotton (but there is MSP for cotton). The prices were controlled by the local vendors. Also, there was no system to sell the crops to the government. For potatoes, the primary source of demand is Balaji wafers. Farmers store their potatoes in cold storage if the prices are not good. They do not think there is MSP for potatoes.

Two focus groups discussions from Boriyavi, Anand, gave a different perspective. They said that MSP is present for rice and bajra but it is too low to support the farmers, as even in the case of price crash, they get marginally more than the MSP from the local vendors. This is because if the price of Bajra is low, it is sold as fodder that fetches good price. Also, bajra is a low-cost crop hence there is little risk of making huge losses. If price of rice crashes, they use it to make seeds for the next year. It saves the cost of buying seeds and also provides good output. In short, they have not taken advantage of MSP till now.

4.5.2.2 Sabarkantha

In Sabarkantha, they have MSP for wheat, maize, and cotton. 9 out of 51 farmers (17.64%) told that it is possible to sell the crop to the government. Other 42 farmers (82.35%) told that they never sold their produce to the government, even if there is a MSP. Farmers do not sell to the government because private traders always give them higher price than MSP.

4.5.2.3 Indore

All the 24 farmers of soybean (Indore) informed us that they get higher prices than MSP so soybean is always sold at market price. Government gives good MSP for chana but the government mandis provide good prices anyway so they do not need the MSP.

4.5.2.4 Surat

39 out of the 45 farmers surveyed in Surat had no knowledge about MSP. They have no idea that they can also sell their produce directly to the government if they do not get the proper price. Six educated farmers have some idea about the concept but even they do not know where and how to sell their commodity directly to the government.

For sugarcane in Surat, there are two types of prices that can be declared by the government: State Advised Price (SAP) and Fair and Remunerative Price (FRP). FRP is the minimum price that the factories must pay to the farmers. SAP is supposed to be higher than FRP but of late, it has not been declared at all. The FRP is often higher than the prices actually paid by the factories. However, the farmers have no alternative but to sell to these factories only. There is no establishment that implements the FRP. The factories say that they can give better price to the farmers if they are allowed to produce ethanol from the waste. They are prohibited from doing so at present because Gujarat is a dry state.

For rice, 2 farmers from Surat, aware of MSP, reported that the price of 20 kg bag can be anywhere between Rs. 85–270, when the MSP is Rs. 281. We are told that the quality of rice produced in Surat can be inferior to the one for which the MSP is Rs. 281.

The overall picture that we got from all the villages was that people were hardly aware of the MSP for the crops that they grow. Even if they knew about the MSP, they did not know how to approach the government to sell the crops at that price.

4.5.2.5 Valsad

The selling pattern of fruits and vegetables in Valsad does not give any room for MSP. They sell the produce to the traders even when it has not ripened. They try to get the best prices from the traders themselves.

4.5.2.6 Jodhpur

The price of moong and moth have decreased a little in recent years in Jodhpur but they never went low enough to touch the MSP. 19 farmers who grow other crops feel that the process of selling for MSP is too slow and it takes months to get the money in one's account.

4.5.2.7 Goa

In Goa, the cashew nuts can be sold to horticulture board at the MSP. However, we found that only 11.1% of the surveyed farmers sold their produce there. The remaining sold it either to Goa Bagayatdar (27.7%) or in the open market (61.12%). Farmers say that they get better prices from Bagayatdar or open market than MSP.

The government had set a price of Rs. 8 per coconut in 2014 but none of the farmers we interviewed sold it to the Horticulture Board because they got better prices from the open market. Similarly, rice farmers also report that they get better prices than MSP from the market, hence do not sell to the government.

4.5.2.8 East Godavari

In East Godavari, for rice, farmers get prices which are greater than MSP declared by the government so rice is sold at market price. Farmers with less than 2 acres land preferred selling directly to local traders as soon as the crop is harvested irrespective of the price at that time. They do so in order to avoid any additional transportation charges and also they do not have proper storage facilities to store their yields. Farmers with more than 3 acres have been storing their yields and sell only when the price is good. They too sell directly to local traders. The reason for this was said by farmers that the procedure is very tedious and the amount is also not transferred instantly.

4.5.2.9 Conclusion

In East Godavari, Goa, Jodhpur, and Indore, farmers are aware of MSP. However, they receive the same price or higher from traders to they do not bother about MSP. Also in East Godavari and Jodhpur we were informed that the money transfer takes a very long time if you sell to the government at MSP. It is not worth the trouble.

In Valsad, Surat, Sabarkantha, Kheda and Anand, many crops grown did not have MSP. Even if they did, most farmers in Kheda, Anand, Valsad, and Surat did not have much knowledge about MSP. They did not even know how the produce can be sold to the government. Some knowledgeable farmers knew about it but they felt that the MSP was usually lower than the market price that they received.

4.5.3 Compensation from the Government

The government tends to pay compensation to all the farmers whose crop production has been adversely affected, whether they were insured or not. In a few districts, we could gather some information about the compensation paid by the government in the face of a disaster. The farmers, in general, did not seem to be very much satisfied with the compensation amount. They found it to be extremely insufficient.

All farmers except the ones from Umiya farm in Kheda had never received any such compensation from the government. A potato farmer mentioned that they had gotten compensation, that too, in time, but the amount was insufficient. The input cost per acre for Potato is Rs. 80,000–90,000 and the compensation that they got was Rs. 15,000 per acre which was too less to make up for the losses.

In Anand also, in one focus group discussion, all the farmers said that the compensation offered was of practically no value as it failed to cover their losses. Receiving Rs. 1000 per bigha when the input cost is much higher than that and then there is labor cost on top of that. Farmers from Chikhodra felt that the compensation offered does not reach them and is siphoned off by the government workers. Farmers from Boriyavi had a problem with the fact that the compensation is not given in case the loss is affecting only a limited part of the land of a few people. It is offered only when the entire village faces a loss.

In Simla, all the 44 sample farmers reported that they were affected by the hails in 2009 and 2011 when the average production decreased by over 50%. There was no help by anyone and the farmers had to bear the losses. Even when the maize crop was destroyed in 2013 due to heavy rains, there was no compensation given. However, when we talked to the Agriculture Department, we found that crop insurance was given to some 3000 apple farmers in 2009 and their claims were also disbursed. The number of insurance holders and claims were higher in 2011. Maybe our sample farmers were not covered by these schemes.

Twenty-six farmers around Prantij area (south Sabarkantha) were hit by heavy rain a few years ago. Almost the whole crop was ruined but they received no help from the government. Only three farmers got insurance money but it was not enough: one farmer reported to have gotten 1500 rupees only, it is the same as no help. One farmer from Juna Chamu (Vadali tehsil) said that politics is involved in such compensations: the fund received from the government goes to their voting constituency. Another farmer from the same village added that that gramsevak does not listen to people—when groundnut totally failed in this area in 2013, they applied and asked for help to the government but nobody listened.

4.5.3.1 Conclusion

The above discussion shows why farmers are weary of governmental promises: either they do not receive compensation when they need it or they get too little to compensate for the losses experienced. It is also felt that the rules and regulations are made to exclude as many as possible. Thus, this too has not helped the farmers much.

Chapter 5
Summary and Conclusions

5.1 Learnings from the Secondary Data

5.1.1 Foodgrains

- Among cereals, India's wheat yields are comparable to USA; Punjab and Haryana have yields that are comparable to many developed nations. However, the volatility in yields is somewhat higher—the production risks are higher. But overall the picture is not too dismal. India remains competitive in wheat.
- Both jowar and bajra face almost the similar kind of production risk as other nations but the yields are far too lower compared to other nations. For bajra, there is still some hope because the yields of some districts are higher than even the developed nations but the jowar yields do not paint an encouraging picture at all.
- In rice, India has far lesser competitive advantage: the overall yields are low and volatility is higher. Many regions in India grow rice at extremely low yields. Few states like Tamil Nadu are not able to bring India out of this low level equilibrium.
- Lastly, India has complete disadvantage in growing maize—both yields and volatility compare very poorly with other nations.

The pulse crops in India face comparable risks or lesser than other pulse growing nations but the yields are very low. Pulses have similar record like bajra and jowar—less risk but very low productivity.

Thus we are not very competitive in most foodgrain crops.

A. Parikh, *Risks in Agriculture*, SpringerBriefs in Economics,
DOI 10.1007/978-981-10-6271-1_5

5.1.2 Cash Crops

- Some districts have good cotton yields—although not as high as USA—but in general the average Indian yields are far lower with much higher volatility.
- Cotton is an important export crop for us; yet the yields are very low compared to our competitors. We need to address this problem soon.
- India is competitive in tobacco—yields are comparable to the USA and the volatility is also not much higher. But whether we want to encourage more cultivation of this crop is an ethical issue.
- The sugarcane yields are somewhat lower but not worrisome. The volatility is also comparable. We seem to have some competitive edge here.
- India is known to be inefficient in oilseeds and our data for ground nut and soybean also reveal the same trend—low yields and very high volatility. We are not competitive in this crop.

5.1.3 Horticulture Crops

- Although potato is a very popular vegetable among Indians, India is very poor in growing potatoes. The yields are half of the USA and fluctuations are 2–4 times more.
- Cashew nuts yields are abysmally low.
- On the contrary, India is competitive in coconut and apples.

The overall agriculture conditions require attention because the scenario is not very encouraging. Farmers need to be given access to irrigation and understanding of appropriate methods for growing crops. We found that farmers are able to access quality seeds. They did not complain much about plant diseases and pests thus indicating that they have satisfactory access to pesticides. The major problems seem to be water and in some places, labor.

5.2 Learnings from the Field Survey

5.2.1 The Risk Profile

The main factors emerging as risks from the field survey were as follows:

- 73% of the farmers identified weather—excessive or untimely rains, hailstorms and extreme change in temperatures—as the most important risk that they face. It can result in 10–15% production loss or it could destroy the whole crop.

- 57% farmers said that animals (pigs, neelgai, rats, etc.) pose a serious threat to their crops. Here also the damage could be up to 80–90%, although usually it seems to be 30–40%.
- 28% farmers felt that pests presented a serious hazard for their crops. The rest felt that pesticides enable them to take care of the pests and even if there are some pests, the damage is not much. From their description, the losses seem to be generally 10–20% of the production.
- Farmers seem to be more or less satisfied with the seeds' and other inputs' quality.

5.2.2 *Price Risk*

As far as price risk is concerned, Ramesh Chand (2003) notes that for most of the crops and in most of the states, MSP is only notional. Our survey shows that only about 10% of the farmers have used it sometimes. None of the sample farmers from nine districts ever used MSP. Many did not even know how one can sell at MSP to the government. The farmers also believed that prices received by them from traders are usually higher than the MSP.

The more disturbing finding is that the farmer is usually given the minimum possible price—it is close to the local minima; therefore fluctuations in prices that go above the local minimum points do not affect the farmers much. It affects the players higher up in the supply chain, i.e., the brokers, wholesale and retail traders, ginning mills, etc. The farmer is *always* at a disadvantage.

Potatoes, which we found was a preferred crop for the large compared to small farmers, showed a peculiar preference design: The producers counted average profits over 3–4 years to decide the performance of the crop. The year to year variability, they say, is taken care of when you take average profits over 3–4 years. The long term price pattern with these moving averages has been quite stable, according to them.

The observations of farmers from different districts make it clear that it is not so much the price fluctuations that we need to worry about; it is the low level of prices received by the farmers that is more of a worry.

5.2.3 *Insurance*

Only 36% of the farmers from our sample 527 farmers had insurance. Most farmers thought that (a) they do not need insurance because their production risks are manageable; (b) the procedures would be too cumbersome and there would be too much paper work. None of them had any appetite for it; (c) they argued that even if one gets insurance cover, there is no guarantee that they would get money in case of crop loss because there would be too much paper work to claim insurance; (d) Even if the insurance can be claimed, the returns would be too little; and (e) There is a possibility that in case of individual loss, the government would not even consider it as a loss.

In short, there is no faith in the government or its policies.

5.3 Lessons from Russia (Taken from the Annexure)

India followed the Russian model of development. For agriculture development also, the independent India first focused on cooperative movement (just like kolkhoz, the collective farms). The yields in Soviet Union were always higher and less volatile compared to India. It is interesting to examine how Russia achieved it.

As education was made compulsory at primary level and higher education was made free, USSR could train its workforce adequately. Agriculture scientists were trained for the new technology for each crop. The experts on agriculture were then sent to work in various regions. The government decided where each graduate would be sent so it was easier to ensure that all regions are covered. As the number of experts increased, the dissemination of technology became better and wide spread. Extension activities in India have never been so strong; this is one point where we seem to have lost out.

As USSR started making heavy machinery, it provided the farms with tractors, harvesters and other equipment. It also provided seeds and fertilizers at low prices. In 1958 agriculture sector in Russia had more than a million tractors—nearly 2 times more than in 1950; more than half a million of harvesters—2.5 times more than in 1950. For the best use of these machines, the government hired tractor drivers, combine operators, and mechanics. Also government created a network of agricultural schools, which prepared the farm machinery operators. Thus training, education, and provision of quality inputs made the production increase.

The developed states of India (like Punjab or Gujarat) have developed a market for hired services of machines and machine operators or even for buying irrigated water (pumps are hired for an hour). Unfortunately, not all states have been able to develop such markets, thus they could not take advantage of the modern technology.

Prices were predetermined by the government; market was not allowed to operate. Although this was often found to be restrictive by the farmers, it ensured that there was no undue loss of income for them.

The insurance was made compulsory for all Russian farmers; premium was heavily subsidized by the government. Mainly natural hazards were covered but the important thing was, all farmers were fully compensated by the system; there was no denial of claim. Indemnity was paid even to the farmers who had not paid the premium. This must have won the trust of farmers. Such efficient reimbursement could work wonders. This practice also helped in stabilizing the returns for the agriculture sector as a whole. Stability provided a solid foundation for growth.

In short, USSR taught modern technology to its farmers, built extensive irrigation network, made available good quality inputs and then protected them also in case of natural disasters. Such combined approach took USSR to a higher level of agriculture output: in five years, 1954–1958, the production increased by 1.5 times. This is what we need to learn from them: teaching the use of technology and making it accessible to farmers.

The capitalist model of insurance, introduced after the disintegration of USSR, has not worked well in Russia either. The main problems:

- The premiums are high, claims are not honored many times, compensation is negligible compared to the total losses. In 2015 crop losses in 25 regions amounted to 1.5 billion rubles, but only RUB 991.1 million were paid as indemnities. Companies made handsome profits because the claims were not paid.
- For making claims, the threshold of losses itself is too high—so high that farmers in the naturally endowed regions would hardly ever make such losses. Knowing that the probability of being compensated is low, the farmers have stopped taking insurance cover. This gave rise to adverse selection.
- The weather data itself is not reliable now so both companies and farmers can be at loss.
- The method of counting average production for last five years can lead to very misleading figures—what if two of those five years were drought years?
- Using last year's price also has the same disadvantage—what if it was bumper crop and the prices had crashed?

Due to all these reasons, insurance coverage has declined to just 10.9% of the total acreage. Thus, India does not have much to learn from the capitalist Russian model. The inherent basic principles of the Soviet system of mandatory agri-insurance hold out interesting lessons though: the mass participation of farmers, which allowed to distribute the risks; nonprofit insurance; indemnity guarantees; and single insurance fund.

5.4 Conclusion

If we compare the two main risks that the farmers face, our data shows that the farmers feel the production risks are far more serious than the price risks. Unfortunately the reason for not feeling the brunt of price fluctuations is not assured protective and remunerative prices but prices received at such low levels that they anyway receive only the lowest prices of the fluctuation cycle. Our marketing system needs to be made far more efficient if we want the price rise gains to reach the farmers.

Production risks are almost always borne by the farmers themselves. At times, the losses are too high, but usually they weather it by not relying too much on agricultural incomes alone. This too is not a desirable situation. We found that better use of technology and accessibility to protective irrigation can make the production fluctuations far lesser. Some innovative solutions for disseminating technology can make the production reach new heights. India needs to concentrate on making modern but simple technological solutions available to farmers.

An important risk factor that emerged from the discussions with farmers that is seldom discussed in policy circles is animals. Animals seem to present a serious threat to crops. This should be a relatively easier problem to address that can increase our productivity at least by 20–30%. We need to develop simple fences, sensors and alarms and other affordable solutions for this problem, since they seem to be affecting farmers all over India.

Insurance will not be attractive to farmers till efforts are made to build some faith in the government system. Only after the farmers are properly and promptly compensated for losses after a natural disaster, the interest can increase. The paper work should be minimized, claims registration should be prompt and easy (some agent should facilitate it after disaster), and the indemnity should be of acceptable proportion. Unless serious effort goes into building such a network, our survey shows that people would not be interested in insurance or feel more secure because of it.

Annexure 1
Agriculture insurance in Russia

Anastasiya Nazarova

Russian Federation belongs to the countries with the riskiest agriculture conditions. Due to the frequent adverse natural events, a large part of the Russia acreage locate in the risky agriculture zone. It is recognized that in the south of Russia desperately dry years cycle 25 times during 30 years, temperate dry years cycle one time during 3–4 years. Each year some part of agricultural producers carries enormous losses from natural disasters. In many regions 3–5 years during ten years usually are lean. Yield fluctuations reach 30–50% of the normal annual average. The most yield volatility inherent to the grain-crops. Fluctuations in the production of livestock are less noticeable (Fig. 1).

Because of high agriculture riskiness agriculture insurance actuality in Russia is also high. Throughout the Russian history, the most effective system of compulsory agricultural insurance existed in the Soviet Union. If before revolution of 1917 it was existed only mutual and «zemsky» insurance, which covered constructions and buildings from hail and fire, then after 1917 year it was started the strong system of agriculture insurance formation.

First of all it's worth to say some words about after revolution and after war economy recovery because it'll help to clarify the agriculture situation, ideas, political trends, government aspirations and the very core of the economy building during those years.

After the 1917 revolution all the lands were nationalized and given in free use to farmers (toiling masses). Farmers received more than 150 million ha in addition to that they owned early.

On Lenin's initiative it was carried out the transition to the New Economic Policy (NEP), providing stronger link between industry and agriculture thanks to wider use of commodity-money relations. If before revolution farmers had to **surrender all of production, after 1917 it was entered tax in kind**, amounted to 50–70% of the production and was surrendered by fixed state prices. Also State regulated the crops, which must be produced. Fixed prices were low. It was compensated by preference price on scarce industrial goods. Farmers had a right to

A. Parikh, *Risks in Agriculture*, SpringerBriefs in Economics,
DOI 10.1007/978-981-10-6271-1

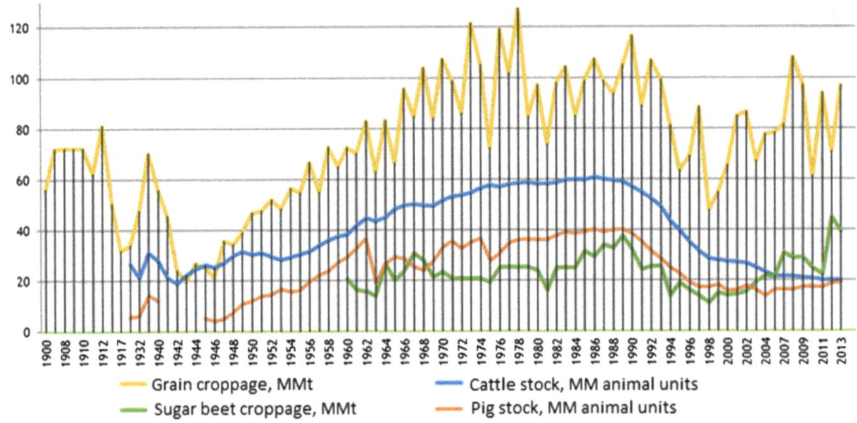

Fig. 1 The main agriculture products dynamics in 1900–2013 years

sell surplus production on the market. The ownership on the output created an incentive for planting and increasing production. Products surrender was strictly controlled. Violators were punished strictly. Rich peasants («kulak») were ruined and exiled to Siberia.

After the 1917 revolution the government insurance system of agencies—«Gosstrah SSSR», was put in place which had a monopoly on all types of insurance. As an exception, cooperatives were allowed to carry out insurance on a mutual basis. All operations were divided into compulsory tax insurance and voluntary insurance. It was mandatory to insure horses, cattle, private homes and crops. Assured could insure the same objects "over a tax"—up to the full value of the insured object.

Insurance coverage was different in different history periods. Till 1967 it was implementing compulsory tax insurance (production, constructions, animals were insured in fixed sums (amounts). For example in 30s grains was insured within 50 rubles/ha, potatoes—180 rubles/ha. Premium rates were established in terms of Soviet republics. For example for RSFSR crops insurance against hail valued at 1.15 rubles/100 rubles of sum insured, against winterkill—2.10 rubles/100 rubles of sum insured.

The industry and cities development required more and more bread and other products from agriculture. Small farmers couldn't provide all of country food demand. That's why to provide economy of scale, the government set a course for collectivization through creating cooperatives named «kolkhoz» (collective farms) and «sovkhoz» (state farms).

In 1927 it was already more than 10 thousand of collective farms. Still it was existed extensive network of primary cooperatives. Through these years the undeveloped lands were reclaiming, cereals, meat and dairy factories were building. In 1929 the average area of cereal factories was near 100 thousand ha.

As a result of total agriculture collectivization in the 30s, socialistic property became the basis of economic relations in the countryside.

In a short time illiteracy in the countryside was basically eliminated. Courses were made to work on agricultural staff preparation (agronomists, livestock experts, tractor specialists, drivers and others). An important role in the collective farms formation and strengthening played a state financial assistance and organizational support of the working class.

The new technical base was prepared for large-scale socialist agricultural production. Mass production of tractors and agricultural machinery was undertaken. The state machine and tractor stations network (MTS) organization also contributed to the technical equipment of agriculture development.

In 1940, there were 236.9 thousand of collective farms, 4.2 thousand of state farms and 7.1 thousand of MTS. Some collective farms weren't served by MTS. For such ones it was stated reduced rates of grain surrender. Co-operation, the agricultural machinery development, increasing number of qualified staff encouraged the agricultural production sound increase (Table 1). In 1940 the total agricultural production has increased in comparison with 1921 by 135%. The crop yields and livestock productivity increased.

In 1940 the insurance coverage was increased: for example grains was insured within 60 rubles/ha, potatoes—250 rubles/ha. Premium rate on hail insurance was 1.25 rubles/100 rubles of sum insured, against winterkill—3.5 rubles/100 rubles of sum insured.

After The Great Patriotic War (1941–1945) five-year plan (1946–1950) of national economy recovery was formulated. In accordance with this plan vegetable and livestock bases were made around the cultural, commercial centers and other major cities for the purpose of providing these centers with vegetables, potatoes, milk and meat.

In 1945 the USSR Council of People's Commissars issued decree on rural electrification development. For illumination of the huts, mills operations, stockyards water supply, carpentry and mechanical workshops and so on it were built hydropower, wind-driven stations and thermal power electric driven stations in the collective and state farms, near the machine-tractor stations. The rural electric power stations developed quickly (Table 2).

Until 1948, the fight against drought waged mainly by the snow accumulation on the fields in winter that prevented snow blowing to the ravines, and the detention of spring meltwater. These measures didn't have a big influence on the risks.

In this context government made the long-term investment to recovery and expansion of the state tree windbreaks, which were to protect the Central Asia prairies from the pernicious influence of hot winds. The introduction of grass crop rotation and construction of ponds and reservoirs helped to reduce the droughts risk.

Investment efficiency from setting water channels on the Amu-Darya River and between the Volga and Don Rivers, and setting three hydroelectric power stations on the Volga and Dnieper Rivers for irrigation and watering of lands affected by drought, started showing effect in a few years.

The tough measures for violating grain surrender and frauds continued to act. In 1947, it was enacted the Law "On criminal liability for state and public property

Table 1 Grain crops gross collection in 1913–1938, MM centner

	1913	1922	1928	1929	1930	1931	1932	1933	1934	1935	1936	1937	1938
Grain crops gross collection, MM centner	801.0	562.7	733.2	717.4	835.4	694.8	698.7	898.0	894.0	901.0	827.3	1202.9	949.9

Table 2 Rural electric power stations development in USSR during 1945–1950

	1945	1946	1947 plan	1950 plan	1950 fact
Electrified collective farms number	12,984	15,400	22,013	70,000	–
Rural stations power (kilowatts)	340,000	382,000	–	1,800,000	770,000

theft". Nestled harvest was considered stolen. It was promised the criminal responsible for such actions.

Despite the five-year plan measures, agriculture continued to suffer a great shortage of tractors and other agricultural machines. There was poorly developed farm practices. There wasn't enough fertilizer, that limited the possibility of increasing the yield. The development of agricultural production was also hampered by weak material interest of collective farms and farmers to increase agricultural production (because of law fixed prices).

To the end of 50s, when the fifth five-year plan was realized, the level of education was raised and a lot of agriculture specialists was directed to the rural area for a work. But there weren't special compulsory trainings for farmers. They of course can take the experience from newly arrived specialists.

In 1953 the Government planed a number of measures aimed to strengthening the collective and state farms, to the rise in agricultural production. Thanks to increasing number of heavy industry, it was possible to provide the rural areas with large number of tractors, combines, machines and other agricultural equipment. In 1958 agriculture had more than a million tractors—nearly 2 times more than in 1950; more than half a million of harvesters—2.5 times more than in 1950.

For the best use of these machines it was hired tractor drivers, combine operators, machinists to MTS. Also it was created a network of agricultural schools, which prepared the farm machinery operators.

For five years (1954–1958) state invested in agriculture mechanization 2.5 times more than in the previous five years. It was sent 120 thousand of specialists to the MTS, collective and state farms.

To raise the material interest of collective farms and farmers to increase agricultural production, the government had increased purchase prices to the extent ensured profitability. In this regard, the collective farms revenues had increased. The collective farms were given the right to decide what crops to produce. In the 50s years it was intensified patronage assistance of the city over the country-side. Factories staff helped collective farms to introduce mechanization in livestock farming.

Collective farms had their own seeds funds. If it wasn't sufficient they bought additional seeds from government funds at the state established price. Or, if they didn't have enough money, they could take noninterest natural loan (in seeds). What about fertilizers—also it weren't free product.

Among the most important Party and the state activities, aimed to the increasing the grain production, the development of virgin and long-fallowed lands in the country east played special role. It was brought many powerful tractors and other machinery to these areas. The Party appealed to the Communists, young people, agriculture machine operators to go to develop virgin lands. The power of ideology was very strong in the country. It is worth to quote a saying of a employee of virgin land letter: "The soul is happy when you see the desert turns into a blooming land. I am proud that my modest share of the labor is invested to this great national goal".

In 1954–1956 36 million ha of virgin and fallow lands were mastered. It was created more than 400 new state farms on these grounds. The virgin lands development had increased grain production significantly. For example, in Kazakhstan in 1958 it was procured about 950 million pounds—6.5 times more than in 1953. Within five-year period (1954–1958) agricultural production had increased by more than 1.5 times.

The majority of farms became stronger and was able to purchase the necessary equipment without appealing to the MTS services. Qualified organizers of production, machine operators were able to use modern agricultural techniques skillfully.

In 1958 the USSR Supreme Soviet adopted the law on MTS reorganizing into repair and engineering stations (RTS). Its tractors, combines and other equipment were sold to the collective farms. After uniting the land and the necessary equipment for its cultivating in one hand the collective farms became to use agricultural machinery more effectively.

In 1968 it was introduced collective farms («kolkhoz») compulsory state insurance, the tax insurance continued to operate for private households. The state farms («sovhoz») were not the subject of compulsory insurance. Mandatory state insurance for state farms was introduced only in 1978.

Since 1967 the Law on state compulsory insurance of collective farm's property was put in place. Fixed sums were removed. Collective farms were indemnified on the 60% of crop losses value; and 70% of animal losses value. Premium rates were 7–10% of planed insurance value accounted the next way: government purchasing price times five-years average yield. It varied depending on crop and region.

Only natural hazards risks were insured in the system of compulsory agri-insurance. There weren't price or income insurance, as well as in modern Russia. There was only production insurance. The prices were fixed, but they were quite low.

We can see some main trends in soviet compulsory agricultural insurance development: agricultural insurance institutionalization strengthening, the increase in the list of objects of insurance, expanding the range of insurable risks, the increase in tariffs, insurance rates and farm operations results correlation strengthening, insurance rates differentiation deepening, the expansion of additional state assistance in case of large disasters.

Compulsory insurance was perpetual. Reinsurance functions were performed by Inter-republican reserve fund. It gave loans to the Soviet republics in case of lack of their inside funds for compensation. During 1970–1990 Republican insurance funds fully compensated farmer's losses with the exception of the loss in extremely adverse weather conditions in 1975 and 1981, when it was used Inter-republican reserve fund. There was no one denial of claim.

Indemnity was paid regardless of whether farmer made a payment or not. The insurance rates were based on the average size of crops damage within every region for the previous 10 years, and for farm animals—5 years.

Insurance rates were recounted at least once every five years. Thus, it is implementing the principle of non-profit insurance business.

Any excess of revenues over expenditures for state compulsory insurance was used only for the indemnities in future years when the funds of the current year won't be enough.

Insurance Fund for compulsory insurance was distributed as follows: for the indemnities—91%, to preventive measures—4%, to inter-republican reserve fund—3% and for government insurance agencies maintenance, mass—raising work—2%. The government statutorily prescribed the list of necessary preventive measures paid a great attention to it.

All of the Republics belongs to one country—USSR where there was government monopoly on almost everything, it was centralized management, command economy. So all of its regions had equal rights and followed uniform government rules. It was the one insurance fund and uniform insurance rules too.

Higher education was not obligatory, but it was free. There also existed post-graduate work assignment system. After graduation from the university specialist was selectively placed to work in his or her specialty (often not to home region) for 3–5 years. It was obligatory for agriculture specialties too. So many experts remained to work in agriculture.

Public-social ideology, aimed to maximizing crop yields, also affected the efficiency of insurance. There was the battle for the harvest. Farmers strive to over-fulfill the plan. It was the ideology. Insurance guaranteed possibility of reproducing in the case of bad weather. But insurance was necessary not so much for farmers as for Party and State. Government was interested in high yields, because it allowed to store more production and use it for meeting town consumers demand and for export.

For the years of Soviet power it was made a great work on agriculture technical providing. The growth in volumes was accompanied by quantum growth. The main agricultural production assets increased by 11.6 times throughout 1941–1975 years. In the Soviet Union there was very strong technical base.

Present Situation

But nowadays there is a low technology level of agriculture. Soviet technology park is outdated and its renewal is very slow. Coefficient of tractors renewal was only 3.1% in 2014, coefficient of grain harvesters renewal—5.2%. Russian machinery is distressed. Modern innovative technology of foreign manufacturers is available only to large and some medium-sized farms, as about small businesses—technology park is outdated.

However, farmers are increasingly using mineral fertilizer in production process. During 2000–2014 years the application of mineral fertilizers per hectare had doubled. It affects also on agriculture insurance.

After the USSR breakup compulsory insurance was cancelled, effective system of agricultural insurance had collapsed. Insurance was taken over by private business, which did not have sufficient insurance funds to cover high agricultural risks. The rules of agricultural insurance government support was changing from year to year, not allowing the system to stabilize.

Nowadays government supports voluntary crop and livestock agri-insurance through subsidizing premium at the level of 50%. On another hand such subsidy may be obtained by the farmer in some stated conditions. Agricultural insurance government support in Russia is regulated by Federal law № 260-FZ "On state support in the field of agricultural insurance". Thus, farmers must be insured only in commercial companies—members of Agri-insurance national union. This Union forms compensation payments fund using 5% member premiums deductibles. The fund is to indemnify farmers who were insured in later insolvent insurer.

Insured event in the sphere of crops is loss of harvest equal to 20% of average harvest (non-deductible franchise). Producer can choose the level of deductible franchise (from 0 to 30%) according to its possibilities and goals. In the sphere of livestock insurance it's covered events of mortality and forced slaughter. Government states vast range of risks that can be insured with its support. For example crops can be protected against natural risks (atmospheric, soil drought, frost, winterkill, damping-off, hail, dust storm, ice crust, flood, flooding, landslides, waterlogging of the soil, strong wind, hurricane, earthquake avalanche, mudflow, wildfires); penetration and (or) the spread of harmful organisms; violation of electricity, heat and water supply as a result of natural disasters.

But farmer doesn't have a right to choose the set of risks: all insurance contracts include a single indivisible set. Also the Federal law fixes rage of crops and animals which can be insured. As for crops: cereals, legumes, oilseeds, technical, fodder, melons, potatoes, vegetables, vines, fruit, small fruit, nut plantations, plantations of hops, tea. As for livestock: cattle (buffaloes, bulls, oxen, cows, yaks); small livestock (goats, sheep); pigs; horses, asses, mules and donkeys; the camels; deer (deer, spotted deer, reindeer); rabbits, fur-bearing animals; bird egg-laying breeds and poultry meat species (geese, turkeys, chickens, quail, duck, guinea fowl), broiler chickens; bee family.

If the difference between expenses and income from agricultural insurance is more than 5% of income, then this difference go to stabilization reserve using for future indemnities.

The share of the insured acreage is decreasing. In 2016 it was insured only 5% of planted acreage (in 2014—17.7%; 2015—10.9%). Number of insured households is reducing. Insurance is not in demand with the farmers thanks to majority of cause. Mainly it's because of premiums onerousness and difficulties with indemnities obtaining due to deductibles and unfair practices of insurance companies.

There is high concentration of agri-insurance market in Russia. Top-5 of 43 insurance companies accumulated near 45% of total premium amount in crop insurance. As well, Top-5 of 22 insurance companies accumulated near 72% of total premium amount in livestock insurance. The government support doesn't apply to mutual and cooperative insurance.

During 2015–16 it was managed insurance companies sanctioned by Russian financial regulator—The Bank of Russia. As a result many troubled insurers licenses were revoked (17 insurance companies).

The loss of ratio has been going down from 78.2% in 2003 to 11.4% in 2015. In 2015 it was announced crop losses in 25 regions in the amount of 1.5 billion rubles. But it was indemnified only RUB 991.1 million. The total premiums were almost nine times higher than total indemnities. Author's calculations showed, that for the 2001–2014 period the loss ratio (indemnities/premiums) amounted near 50%. It underlines that government subsidies don't come down to agricultural producers in fact.

The total sum insured under insurance contracts submitted for subsidies was 155.8 billion rubles, total insurance premiums—8.9 billion rubles (212.6 and 12.5 billion rubles in 2014 respectively). The average rate of insurance amounted to 5.71% (2014—5.89%).

In 2015 5367.6 million rubles subsidies were included into the federal budget for state agricultural insurance: 4910.1 million rubles for crop insurance (spent funds—3877.6 million rubles or 78.2%), 457.5 million rubles for Livestock insurance (spent funds—362.3 million rubles, or 78.2%). 402.8 million rubles were transferred from the local budgets of the Russian Federation regions.

In 56 constituent entities of the Russian Federation (from the 85) it's subsidized 3619 crop insurance contracts on the total area of 8.3 million hectares and to total insured amount of 155.8 billion rubles.

Insured acreage leaders among regions were Republic of Tatarstan, Krasnodar region, Stavropol region, Orenburg region, Kursk region.

51 region participated in the program of livestock insurance. It was insured 17.9% of total livestock. Average insurance rate amounts to 1.06% (in 2014—1.21%). Indemnities under contracts of insurance have not been made, the losses were not declared.

The government support doesn't have sufficient influence on insurance activity of farmers. The low level of insured agriculture production caused by range of factors.

Government doesn't establish the official goal of agricultural insurance with the government support or the goal of agricultural insurance government support.

Agri-insurance government support is carried out under "Risk management in crops and livestock farming" measure, which is a part of Government program of agricultural development for 2013–2020. This program specifies the expected result of realizing such measure is reduction risks of revenue losses during crops and animals producing.

On the other hand, in the "National report about government program of agricultural development realizing" the risk reducing measures goal sounds as reducing negative effects associated with adverse natural character events.

Alternatively, subsidy using efficiency is appreciated by the Ministry of agriculture of the Russian Federation every year with reference to the percentage of insured planting acreage and to the percentage of insured farm animals through all the country.

Federal law "On state support in the field of agricultural insurance" certainly doesn't hold the goal of government support.

So, it isn't clear why the government supports agricultural insurance.

Government support cover only natural and biological hazards insurance, but doesn't cover market risks such as price fluctuations.

Despite of 50% premium government support, the value of insurance policies still remains very expensive.

In spite of non-deductible franchise was adjusted from 30 to 20% for last three years, such losses threshold remains enough high for many regions with good natural conditions. Moreover this threshold is also not «achievable» for innovative, technological farmers. Realizing the low probability to get indemnity, farmers recognize unreasonable to pay high valued premiums. Agri-insurance with government support loses a sense for such farmers. So, the adverse selection arouse.

Another enormous problem is inadequate insurance rates. Government fixed the marginal subsidized rates for each crop or crop groups but common for every region. Insurance companies have a right to stand individual for every producer rate. But generally they use marginal subsidized rates. In result some insurance contracts are overpaid and others underpaid. There isn't sole confirmed methodology of insurance rate evaluating.

The current method of harvest insurance value determining also have some disadvantages. Now it's appreciated using five-years average yield and last year price. And it doesn't take into account the years of anomalous weather with anomalous harvest. Such years are included in the five years average yield. So, the insurance value turn out not objective. Also, indemnity is evaluating using last year price too, but taking into account the high rate of inflation in Russia, indemnity come out lower than real value of losses.

Unfortunately, the lack of guidelines for dispute resolution in case of insurance conflicts masks the dispute settlement process.

In addition, low interest of agricultural producers in insurance is due to several factors: low and precarious financial position of many producers; low insurance costs priority compared to direct production costs (for feed, seed, materials, etc.); low farmers insurance culture; low level of agri-insurance state control; underestimation of farmers proposals on agricultural insurance improvement; high transaction costs and uncertainty of getting government subsidies; objective difficulty of crop failure causes identification; underestimation of specific regional risks, insurance companies self elimination from participation in prevented measures organizing (it's connected with unfavorable tax regulation), distrust to insurance companies because of their possible misconduct, underpayments, deviations from indemnities, rigid and excessive demands to technology and so on.

The low interest of insurance companies to agricultural insurance also caused by some factors: the complexity of agricultural insurance evaluating, low insurance culture of farmers, high costs for monitoring agricultural technologies, information asymmetry, low farmers financial possibilities.

The interest decrease of insurance process participants is also affected by the insurance infrastructure imperfection.

Undeveloped weather stations network in different areas causes the lack of reliable data about the weather conditions in particular regions. It does not allow one to determine the true cause and the size of the crop damage. So it forces companies to incur additional expertise costs. Also it leads to delays in the process of indemnifying and reduce their size.

Russian system of federal veterinary Surveillance is not effectively working, that primarily manifested in large outbreaks of avian influenza, African swine fever and so on.

Incomplete statistics on risk events leads to difficulty or impossibility of reliable actuarial risk evaluation.

Existent of different insurance frauds also decrease government support efficiency.

As a result it could be made the conclusion that the inherent basic principles of the Soviet system of mandatory agri-insurance had been lost: the mass participation of farmers, which allowed to distribute the risks; nonprofit insurance; indemnity guarantees (due to the franchise use beginning); single insurance fund; interregional reinsurance; premiums accumulative nature (from year to year). Thanks to these main issues the agricultural insurance in Russia still remains ineffective.

References

Bee Culture (2016) Catch the buzz—top 10 largest sugar producing countries in the world, February 13. http://www.beeculture.com/catch-the-buzz-top-10-largest-sugar-producing-countries-in-the-world/

Binswanger HP (1980) Attitudes towards risk: experiment measurement in rural India. Am J Agric Econ 62(3):174–182

Cotton Corporation of India Ltd. http://cotcorp.gov.in/national-cotton.aspx

Dandekar VM (1976) Crop insurance in India. EPW. Rev Agric 11(26):A61–A80

Ethical Post (2016) Top 10 ground nut producing states in India. December 17. http://www.ethicalpost.in/top-10-groundnut-producing-states-in-india/

Hazell PBR (1982) Instability in Indian foodgrain production. International Food Policy Research Institute, Research report 30, Washington, D.C

IBEF. http://www.ibef.org/exports/cashew-industry-india.aspx

Jodha NS (1981) Role of credit in farmer's adjustment against risk in arid and semi-arid tropical areas of India. EPW XVI (22 and 23)

Mahul O, Stutley CJ (2010) Government support to agricultural insurance : challenges and options for developing countries. World Bank. https://openknowledge.worldbank.org/handle/10986/2432 License: CC BY 3.0 IGO. http://www.mapsofworld.com/world-top-ten/world-map-countries-wheat-production.html

Mahendradev S (1987) Growth and instability in foodgrains production: an interstate analysis. Econ Polit Wkly 22(39):A82–92

National Agriculture Policy 2000. http://rrtd.nic.in/agriculture.html

Nadkarni MV, Deshpande RS (1982) Agricultural growth, instability in productivity and rainfall: case of Karnataka. Econ Polit Wkly 17(52):A127–134

Potatopro.com. The potato sector. http://www.potatopro.com/india/potato-statistics

Raju SS, Chand R (2010) Agricultural risk and insurance in India: problems and prospect. Academic Foundation India

Nair R (2010) Crop insurance in India: changes and challenges. EPW 45(6)

The Hindu (2013). India third largest tobacco producer. http://www.thehindu.com/todays-paper/tp-national/tp-andhrapradesh/india-third-largest-tobacco-producer/article5162698.ece

Toppost.in. http://www.toppost.in/top-10-largest-coconut-producing-states-in-india/

Vyas VS, Singh S (2006) Crop insurance in India. EPW 41:43–44

A. Parikh, *Risks in Agriculture*, SpringerBriefs in Economics,
DOI 10.1007/978-981-10-6271-1

Data

www.agri.goa.gov.in/uploads/
http://apy.dacnet.nic.in/crop_fryr_toyr.aspx
https://data.gov.in/catalog/district-wise-season-wise-crop-production-statistics.
Directorate of economics and statistics, Government of Rajasthan (indiastat.com) faostat.fao.org
Ministry of Agriculture, Government of India (indiastat.com)

MIX

Papier | Fördert gute Waldnutzung

FSC® C083411

Kolibri 360 GmbH
Ferdinand-Jühlke-Straße 7
99095 Erfurt, Deutschland
produktsicherheit@kolibri360.de